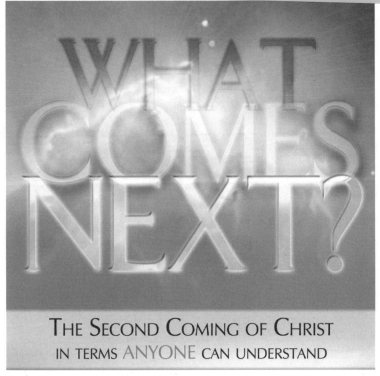

THE SECOND COMING OF CHRIST
IN TERMS ANYONE CAN UNDERSTAND

ROB MICHIE

CREATION
HOUSE
PRESS

WHAT COMES NEXT? by Rob Michie
Published by Creation House Press
A part of Strang Communications Company
600 Rinehart Road
Lake Mary, Florida 32746
www.creationhouse.com

Unless otherwise noted, all Scripture quotations are from the Holy Bible, New International Version. Copyright © 1973, 1978, 1984, International Bible Society. Used by permission.

Cover design by Terry Clifton

Library of Congress Catalog Card Number: 2002104995
International Standard Book Number: 0-88419-891-X

02 03 04 05 87654321
Printed in the United States of America

*To Karen, Ken, Deidre, and Scott for
being great kids and now great
young adults.*

∾

*To Sue, my wife, for putting up with me
while I wrote this and for helping edit
the final version.*

CONTENTS

INTRODUCTION

How do we explain to our children the coming greatest spiritual event of all times—the Second Coming of Jesus Christ?

Some of us ignore the question because we do not understand enough to explain it. Many of us let the clergy educate us as they see fit. Most of us have picked up a little truth and a little fiction here and there. All of us figure we cannot influence the event directly, so why even try and understand it? Who knows when it will happen anyway?

Yet, if this is the next great spiritual event that will result in major changes for our families, shouldn't we be prepared? I believe that all Christians want to be prepared for what comes next.

God has a great plan for the Second Coming, and He has revealed a great deal about it. An enormous portion of both the Old Testament and the

New Testament is dedicated to God's plan and, specifically, the events surrounding the Second Coming.

Many biblical scholars believe that Christ is coming very soon. But is He?

Well, as the father of four wonderful children, I feel called to help them put into perspective the upcoming events foretold in the Bible. Many events in recent times are referenced in the Bible and provide a context to God's plan for mankind. The prophecies of the Bible have been proven accurate in the past and, doubtless, will continue to proven to be true.

In this book, I take on the challenge of understanding, communicating and, to a lesser degree, interpreting the Bible as it relates to the Second Coming. As a Christian father, I want to provide my children with an understanding of God's intentions for us. Those intentions are outlined for us in the Bible, but they are scattered throughout its many books, making it difficult to get an easy understanding of this subject without doing a lot of searching.

My views are mine, but the Bible is the basis upon which I have tried to develop my views. I have formed my opinions over twenty-six years of studying, praying, thinking and listening to others.

The Second Coming is a relevant event to every person on earth. It is an event foretold by Jesus, the Old Testament prophets and the New Testament disciples. Since current events lead many to believe that Jesus will soon return, I trust that this collection of questions and answers will help lead others to a fuller understanding of this great event.

Let me start by sharing a little of the background events leading up to this work on the Second Coming and the inspiration that led to this writing.

In 1975, I was alone in an apartment in Longview, Washington, having just arrived as a new resident. My wife, along with our two oldest children, Karen and Ken, were waiting until I bought a house before they would join me. My temporary residence was a dusty, sparsely furnished apartment, containing a few bare essentials of furniture—just enough to be advertised as "furnished." It was on the second floor of a two-story walk-up overlooking an industrial district of noisy and drab paper and lumber manufacturing mills.

Having just finished five years of service in the U.S. Air Force, I was ready to begin a new career as an industrial engineer, a goal I had worked toward since finishing high school and heading for Texas Tech. I was twenty-seven, full of spunk and ready to be a good engineer in a big corporation located in one of the prettiest parts of the United States. Better still, my family was to join me as soon as I closed on our new house. Life was good!

Besides getting geared up for a new job and getting into the routine it provided, there was not much to do in this part of town. Most of the other apartment residents were transient folks like myself who were gone most of the time. They kept to themselves, leaving me alone to fill the long evening hours.

Being an occasional reader, I searched for a book that was different from the novels I see in airports and pharmacies around the country. As a Christian, I was eager to learn more about the Bible, but I struggled trying to wade through all the ancient history. The Book of Revelation always interested me, but all the weird symbolism made it very difficult to really understand. That's when I found book by Hal Lindsey titled *There Is A New World Coming* (Bantam Books, 1973). For a cost of $1.75, I bought it and took it to my quiet, second-floor apartment.

When I wasn't working on engineering projects I found myself absorbed in the prophecies about the future. For weeks I read and reread the book, and then returned to read the Bible. I joined a local church where my family and I would serve as active members until I was transferred to California. During that time in Longview and in the years since then, I recall the sense of enlightenment I received in my prayerful search and meditation on God's plan for mankind.

As the years passed since 1975, I lived in different cities and towns, and I continued to involve myself in church activities. I volunteered for various positions in different churches. I read the Bible more. I took Bible study courses, and I always remained interested in the prophecies about the future. God provided prophetic messages since early times for people just like me!

Now my sons and daughters range in age from twenty to thirty. All four are Christian young adults living in various places in the U.S. Never have we taken the time to discuss in-depth the proclamations in the Bible about the future. Short conversations never seem to do justice to this important and vibrant topic about which much has been written, much has happened and much is yet to occur.

With four young adults at nearly the same age I was when I went through a period of Christian intrigue, I thought it best for me to organize the things I believe to be true about our future. My hope is that these writings will spur greater faith in the fact that God is working through a master plan. The Second Coming of Christ is ever nearer, and it will be the greatest event the world will witness since His death on the cross, when He conquered sin, and His resurrection.

I asked my sons and daughters to write a few questions they each had about the Second Coming of Christ for me to address in this book. They did so, and to each of those questions I am giving a full explanation from my knowledge of the Bible and my understanding of world events.

This is not a view from an accredited theologian or an extreme religious movement. Trust it to be a simple father's view based on common sense and a deeply felt love for Jesus Christ.

Karen is the oldest of my four children. She is

engaged and lives in Houston, Texas. Ken, my oldest son, lives in Los Angeles where he works as a teacher and a writer. Daughter Deidre graduated from the University of Florida and lives in Houston, Texas, near her sister. Scott is a student at Western Washington University, and he loves surfing in Hawaii, or anywhere else for that matter.

My wife, Sue, and I are blessed that they've all become fine Christian young adults. Sue has been a loving mother and wonderful Christian role model.

Each one of my sons and daughters sent questions to be answered. Each chapter in this book answers a question or a group of similar questions. Some of my answers are relatively short, and others are lengthy.

I hope these questions are tough enough to cause you to search your heart for answers, just as they have made me search my own heart. Important questions deserve time and energy to answer them. Such answers help make up the fundamental beliefs and principles we use to live out our lives. Our words and actions reflect such beliefs and principles, and they ultimately define who we are. In the end, it is our faith and Christ's mercy that open the door to another life in heaven.

May you grow closer to Christ as you think through these questions and answers!

1

THE QUESTION

Growing up in a Christian family, I did all of the ordinary things. I went to Sunday school—even if reluctantly—instead of playing baseball on Sunday mornings with my friends. Under pressure from my parents, I became an altar boy at age twelve in the Episcopal church. But after a year of serving the church, I genuinely accepted Jesus Christ as my Savior.

My newly found faith was largely based on what I was told, which all seemed basically logical. I didn't need any theological training or temptation testing, neither did I need a deep understanding. My simple faith fit nicely into my simple, average life, which was blessed with loving Christian parents.

Over the next ten years I would wrestle with the concept that God could love the world and still stand by and allow the people He created to travel the path of free will. To me, good and bad seemed to coexist in the world, and good didn't necessarily seem to have the upper hand over bad in all cases. I learned that if God truly created us with a free will, He also had to live with the consequences when evil triumphed over goodness. We had to live with it, too!

It was 1966, and I was of age to be drafted during the Vietnam conflict. I wondered how God could allow such a waste of life to continue year after year. It was the same feeling one gets when faced with calamity striking an innocent life. It was the same feeling we all shared as we sat by helplessly watching as terrorists destroyed innocent lives in New York and Washington, D.C. Why would a loving God allow such horrible things to happen?

WHY DOES GOD ALLOW EVIL?

My youngest daughter asked me this question after she received a call during spring break from the University of Florida. Her roommate, a wonderful, gifted Christian, was hit by a truck and killed while simply jogging along a road near her home. A true Christian was lost to everyone who knew her. Why?

Just as we did in the recent terrorist attacks on the U.S., we all grieve over the loss of precious, innocent life. How we deal with that loss and move on is important.

It's essential to understand that God offers salvation throughout eternity following our course in this life. Nevertheless, He does not offer a full package of salvation, protection and freedom from harm during our time here on earth. Our salvation is available through the acceptance of Jesus as our

Savior. Our protection and security is largely based upon the daily choices we make.

In understanding God, we must also understand that God created us in His own image. With that creation comes free will to choose to do goodness or to do evil. People choose to do evil, which is the fault of those particular individuals, not God. People make mistakes that affect others. Some people are lucky, and some are unlucky. God is not responsible for all of that, and we are foolish to think He should be held accountable. We are the ones responsible for our choices and circumstances.

THE PROMISED MESSIAH

For thousands of years the Hebrew people have looked for their coming Messiah. They built their religion, in part, on the expectation that the Messiah would come and free them, protect them and ultimately rule over them as king. Today they continue to wait for the Chosen One.

Jewish teachings tell us of His glorious coming. Yet, most of the Jewish people never have seen Jesus as the Messiah. Even though Jesus came as one of them, they failed to see Him as the central figure in God's plan. God's plan included sacrificing His Son in a manner similar to what God asked of Abraham when the aged patriarch took his son Isaac up a mountain to sacrifice him.

In addition, Jesus did not come surrounded in the trappings of worldly power and wealth as the

Jews expected. Instead, He came in a heavenly display of perfect love, a display they could not see as God's heavenly plan. Instead they saw Jesus as a teacher and a prophet. The Jewish nation could not accept Jesus Christ as their true Savior.

How often do our own expectations run ahead of what God is doing and saying? It is our nature to run ahead of God. I do it, and sitting here in the twenty-first century, I can easily see how the Hebrews did it two thousand years ago.

Yet, those of us who are Christians and who are attempting to steer our children to faith in Jesus Christ do see Jesus as the Messiah. He has come as the loving Savior with wisdom and understanding beyond anyone before or after Him. His miracles and His Word witness to His truth as God's Son.

Bible prophecies are recorded for us, and they foretell many events in human history. Most of the Bible prophecies have already been fulfilled. Those yet to come center around the Second Coming of Christ.

As a Christian parent, I have found it difficult to talk with my sons and daughters about this event and what surrounds it. Our church life and the spiritual life that accompanies it center on worship, prayer, thanksgiving, Bible study, fellowship, charity and volunteerism. The Second Coming is lightly discussed at best.

ANSWERING QUESTIONS ON THE SECOND COMING

I promised my sons and daughters a timely and

thoughtful response to their questions about the Second Coming. Answering their questions required much more work than I expected, I sorted their questions into eight groups. Next, I researched the Bible for answers. Third, I answered the questions using the Bible and my own common sense. Hopefully, my responses will help all four of these great young adults to become better Christians.

In researching my answers, I felt like a shepherd caring for his flock. I claim no special place and no greater insight than anyone else. My answers are based on my beliefs, my experiences and my under- standing of the Word of God. My hope is that anyone who considers what is written here does so with joy in his or her heart for what God has offered us through His Son Jesus Christ.

The following are the eight groups of questions and answers. A separate chapter of this book is dedicated to each.

2

SIGNS

To my daughter Karen: I chose to answer one of your questions first because it is at the chronological beginning of the entire prophetic message of the Second Coming.

You asked, "The Bible talks about signs that lead to the coming of Christ. How many of these signs have we seen?"

Both the New and Old Testaments mention signs surrounding the Second Coming of Christ. Let me address those in the New Testament with which I am familiar. Then, I will comment on the Old Testament.

Keep in mind that Jesus was very sensitive about revealing signs of His divinity to others. Those who believed in what He said got His attention, and to them He revealed much about Himself and about the future. But to those who did not believe, such doubters were unworthy of such precious revelation. In the Book of Mark we read:

> The Pharisees came and began to question Jesus.

> To test him, they asked him for a sign from heaven. He sighed deeply and said, "Why does this generation ask for a miraculous sign? I tell you the truth, no sign will be given to it."
>
> —MARK 8:11–12

How often do we ask for a sign from God? Hopefully, our faith is strong enough not to test Jesus as the Pharisees did. If we believe, we will be rewarded for that faith. One of the rewards that we get in this generation is an opportunity to understand some of the signs of the End Times given by Jesus to His disciples.

Importantly, in Matthew 16 Jesus predicted His own death to His disciples. At the same time, He also predicted His own return:

> For the Son of Man is going to come in his Father's glory with his angels, and then he will reward each person according to what he has done.
>
> —MATTHEW 16:27

If you believe in the authority of Jesus Christ, then you have His Word that He will indeed return. His Word is greater than a sign. It is His establishment of a truth. Throughout the Gospels, Jesus carefully fulfills the Old Testament prophecies, and He declares new truths about the future.

Second, He promises rewards in heaven. Nevertheless, salvation comes first, and rewards come second. I'll discuss more about these rewards in a later chapter on judgment.

In the Book of Matthew, while in Jerusalem Jesus begins telling us of the end of time:

> Jesus left the temple and was walking away when his disciples came up to him to call his attention to its buildings. "Do you see all these things?" he asked. "I tell you the truth, not one stone here will be left on another; everyone will be thrown down."
>
> —MATTHEW 24:1–2

The Romans destroyed that temple and much of Jerusalem too in A.D. 70. The Jewish temple has never been rebuilt, as of yet. Therefore, Jesus correctly prophesied the temple's destruction. He gave no specific timeframe as to when the Second Coming might occur in respect to that razing of the temple.

Notably, since the temple was destroyed only a few decades after Jesus' death, many early Christians thought that this was a sign that His coming was imminent or would happen in the next few years. For some, hope grew into frustration as Christians suffered much persecution in those years. Some, no doubt, lost faith. Fortunately, many others carried the truth of the gospel message forward. To them we owe thanks for the continued growth of the church. Without these faithful first-century saints, our church family would be much smaller today.

Jesus continues His discussion of the end of times with the disciples:

> As Jesus was sitting on the Mount of Olives, the

15

disciples came to him privately. "Tell us," they said, "when will this happen, and what will be the sign of your coming and of the end of the age?"

Jesus answered: "Watch out that no one deceives you. For many will come in my name, claiming, 'I am the Christ,' and will deceive many. You will hear of wars and rumors of wars, but see to it that you are not alarmed. Such things must happen, but the end is still to come. Nation will rise against nation, and kingdom against kingdom. There will be famines and earthquakes in various places. All these are the beginning of birth pains."

"Then you will be handed over to be persecuted and put to death, and you will be hated by all nations because of me. At that time many will turn away from the faith and will betray and hate each other, and many false prophets will appear and deceive many people. Because of the increase of wickedness, the love of most will grow cold, but he who stands firm to the end will be saved. And this gospel of the kingdom will be preached in the whole world as a testimony to all nations, and then the end will come."

"So when you see standing in the holy place the abomination that causes desolation, spoken of through the prophet Daniel—let the reader understand—then let those who are in Judea flee to the mountains. Let no one on the roof of his house go down to take anything out of the house. Let no one in the field go back to get his cloak. How dreadful it will be in those days for pregnant women and nursing mothers! Pray that your flight will not take place in winter or on the Sabbath. For then there will be great distress, unequaled from the beginning of the world until now—and never to be equaled again. If those days had not been cut short, no one would survive, but for the sake of the elect those days will be shortened. At that time if anyone says to you, 'Look here is the Christ!' or, 'There he is!' do not believe it. For false Christs and false prophets will appear and perform great signs and miracles to deceive even the elect—if that were possible. See, I have told you ahead of time."

"So if anyone tells you, 'There he is, out in the desert,' do not go out; or, 'Here he is, in the inner rooms,' do not believe it. For as lightning that comes from the east is visible even in the west, so will be the coming of the Son of Man. Wherever there is a carcass, there the vultures will gather."

"Immediately after the distress of those days 'the sun will be darkened, and the moon will not give its light; the stars will fall from the sky, and the heavenly bodies will be shaken.' At that time the sign of the Son of Man will appear in the sky, and all the nations of the earth will mourn. They will see the Son of Man coming on the clouds of the sky, with power and great glory."

—MATTHEW 24:3–30

In Jesus' sermon here in Matthew 24, He warns us of the following signs:

1. False prophets
2. War
3. Famines and earthquakes
4. Persecution
5. Gospel preached throughout the world
6. Desecration of the temple in Jerusalem

7. Unequalled distress in the world leading to near annihilation
8. Dark sun and moon, fallen stars, and a shaken heaven
9. Sign of the Son of Man will appear in heaven
10. All people will mourn and see the Son of Man coming on clouds

I believe that the first five of these signs have occurred and are continuing to occur. The sixth, seventh and eighth signs will be part of the tribulation period that begins seven years before Christ's return. The ninth and tenth signs occur at the end of the tribulation period, the actual time of the Second Coming.

Look at the list above and ask yourself, *Where are we in this prophetic calendar?*

Here's why I believe that the first five signs have already taken place.

- False prophets are evident in many of the major religions in the world today. Many of these prophets have come upon the scene since Jesus' death.

- Major wars have engulfed the world in the past, and many regional conflicts have shattered the peace of our world recently. We have witnessed the proliferation of terrorism in the world following the Gulf War in 1990.

- More earthquakes are occurring than at any other time in recorded history. We even had one recently in Olympia, Washington!
- Famines have plagued Africa throughout recent history. Hunger remains a major concern in many places in Africa and Asia.
- Christians are persecuted throughout the world. In some Muslim nations today, a Muslim can be sentenced to death for converting to Christianity.
- Finally, only in this time period in human history can we truly say that the gospel is available throughout the world. Written materials and various forms of broadcast have taken the Word of God to the most remote regions of the world. Only totalitarian governments keep the Word of God from being available to its citizens!

Therefore, we can safely say the first five events identified by Jesus have happened. In fact, all of them will continue right up to the end.

THE FINAL SIGNS

The remaining signs occur in a relatively short period of time leading up to the Second Coming. The final events of history will involve everyone.

No one will escape the impact of these final days. Jesus makes this clear in the Book of Luke when He discusses the signs of the end of times:

> For it will come upon all those who live on the face of the whole earth.
>
> —LUKE 21:35

One of final events will be the desecration of the Jewish temple. You will see that this temple must be rebuilt for use during the tribulation period. This site is the location of the sixth sign Jesus mentions where the Antichrist will desecrate the temple in the middle of the tribulation period.

Following the temple desecration will be a period of horrible distresses and judgments. These will be the worst of times during the tribulation period occurring over a three and a half year time span. It will end with dramatic changes in the physical heavens. The sky will be darkened and heavenly bodies will be changed. Then the sign of the Son of Man will appear announcing the coming of the Lord.

THE LAWLESS ONE

The apostle Paul tells us another important sign in 2 Thessalonians: Preceding the coming of Jesus Christ, one called the "lawless one" will deceive many people into worshiping him. He is another false prophet against whom we are warned who will not surface until the world enters the tribulation age. The "lawless one" will exalt himself according to Paul:

> Concerning the coming of our Lord Jesus Christ
> and our being gathered to him, we ask you,
> brothers, not to become easily unsettled or
> alarmed by some prophecy, report or letter sup-
> posed to have come from us, saying that the day
> of the Lord has already come. Don't let anyone
> deceive you in any way, for that day will not come
> until rebellion occurs and the man of lawlessness
> is revealed, the man doomed to destruction. He
> will oppose and will exalt himself over everything
> that is called God or is worshiped, so that he sets
> himself up in God's temple, proclaiming himself to
> be God.
>
> —2 THESSALONIANS 2:1–4

Here Paul tells us that the Antichrist must be
revealed to the world before Christ comes back. He
will deceptively lead the world to its destruction.
Until this prophecy is fulfilled, the Second Coming
will wait.

The Book of Revelation tells us much about the
End Times and the tribulation period. It's packed
with powerful symbolism that is often interpreted
differently by many theologians.

Chapters 2 and 3 of the Book of Revelation
describe seven churches in existence at the time
John wrote it. The message to each church precedes a lengthy series of visions of the tribulation
period. The messages also clearly identify many of
the good and bad things experienced in these
churches, which are located throughout Asia
Minor. Interestingly, the messages parallel many of

the same issues experienced by churches today. In fact, the similarities suggest that human nature in organized churches has changed very little since the first century.

In the fourth chapter of Revelation, John recounts hearing a voice say, "Come up here and I will show you what must take place after this" (Rev. 4:1).

With no further mention of the churches, the Lord unveils to John the story of the end of times. He instructs John to tell others of this prophetic message, and He specifically mentions His return in chapter 22, saying:

> Behold, I am coming soon! My reward is with me, and I will give to everyone according to what he has done. I am the Alpha and the Omega, the First and the Last, the Beginning and the End.
>
> —REVELATION 22:12–13

As I see it, the time that the tribulation period begins will mark the end of the church age. The church age was born when the Holy Spirit fell upon the disciples in the upper room at Pentecost. This event permitted anyone who opened his or her heart to Jesus Christ to receive the Holy Spirit. The church has grown through the ages, bringing hundreds of millions to Christ. However, there is to be an end to this church age, and as the gospel message is being heard throughout the world, we are nearing the end of this age and the beginning of the tribulation. We are not there yet, but I believe we are getting close, and I am pleased that you have stayed with Christ. I have faith that you will continue to be discerning of the times in which we live.

OLD TESTAMENT PROPHESIES

The Old Testament prophets told us of the coming of the Messiah, and they predict many events that will precede his appearing. In some passages, it is difficult to separate the description of events about the first coming from the Second Coming. I believe that many of these scriptures relate to both!

Ezekiel, a prophet who lived around 600 B.C., was exiled to Babylon with others of his countrymen. The book of Ezekiel contains pivotal visions about the signs leading to the coming of Christ.

The prophet describes a massive battle that will come against Israel in chapters 38 and 39, but first he tells of the reestablishment of a unified Israel. The Jewish people, according to Ezekiel, must be in possession of their homeland before Christ comes.

We saw this crucial event take place in 1948 when the Jewish people returned to their homeland. In 1967, they expanded their country to include portions of Jerusalem following a six-day war with neighboring Arabs.

This is an amazing historical event in the history of the world. During World War II, forces sought to destroy the Jewish nation through genocide. They had been dispersed throughout the world for centuries with no homeland. Finally, following the unspeakable suffering they experienced under Hitler and the Nazis, they returned to their homeland of Israel under the leadership of the Zionist movement.

The return of the Jews to Israel is the world's most significant sign that events are moving toward Christ's return. Jesus, who was born a Jew, will return to Jerusalem that is inhabited by Jews. It is now in place! Therefore, we can safely say that we have seen that sign come to pass.

PROPHESIES FROM DANIEL

Another Old Testament sign regarding the timing of Christ's return is prophesied in the Book of Daniel. The Book of Daniel was written around 530 B.C. and is fascinating reading. Daniel prayerfully asked God for guidance and earned the right to become a prophet through his excellent lifestyle.

God answered Daniel's questions about the future and about visionary dreams, giving Daniel an extraordinary insight into thousands of years that would follow. Many of the passages interpret his visions of things to come. It is difficult to determine whether these interpretations deal with the first or Second Coming of Christ, or if they possibly deal with both.

Daniel says:

> While I was speaking and praying, confessing my sin and the sin of my people Israel and making my request to the LORD my God for his holy hill— while I was still in prayer, Gabriel, the man I had

seen in the earlier vision, came to me in swift flight about the time of the evening sacrifice. He instructed me and said to me, "Daniel, I have now come to give you insight and understanding. As soon as you began to pray, an answer was given, which I have come to tell you, for you are highly esteemed. Therefore, consider the message and understand the vision:

"Seventy 'sevens' are decreed for your people and your holy city to finish transgression, to put an end to sin, to atone for wickedness, to bring in everlasting righteousness, to seal up the vision and prophecy and to anoint the most holy."

—DANIEL 9:20–24

Daniel had prayed, pleading with God for mercy on the people of Israel. God's answer was delivered by an angel and is recorded in this passage in which he tells Daniel about a plan to end the suffering that will take time. Clearly, as Christians we see that Christ came and died for all who believe. By doing so, He cleared the transgressions committed in the Old Testament, put an end to sin by sacrificing Himself for all our sins and atoned for the wickedness that man brings into the world.

In Daniel's case, it took over five hundred years for the first three purposes to be met. God stopped short of running through the final seven years of tribulation on the Jewish people and the rest of the world. Following Jesus' life a new age was started that allowed the Gentiles to build their church for Christ. When this is done, the end of the church age will signal the start of the final seven years needed to fulfill the Scriptures and bring to a close the Jewish age. It also leads me to believe that God will fulfill the remaining three purposes stated by Daniel at the time of His Second Coming. He will bring in everlasting righteousness, seal up the vision and prophecy and anoint the most holy.

Regarding the timing of the Second Coming, I will address the meaning of the seventy "sevens."

In the Bible, Daniel declares that a couple of interesting events must occur before the coming of the Messiah. In chapter 9, he states that the city of Jerusalem must be rebuilt and restored before the Lord comes. He goes on to mention that the temple will be defiled in Jerusalem.

Interestingly, the city of Jerusalem, which was destroyed prior to the prophecy, was rebuilt after Daniel's prophecy. It was rebuilt centuries before the first coming of Christ. Furthermore, the city was destroyed again shortly after Christ was crucified. Today Jerusalem is rebuilt from work begun in the 1500s. So, the city is rebuilt today and serves as a sign of the Second Coming.

As you can see, just as the Jews have had a difficult history of getting back to their homeland, the city of Jerusalem has had a difficult time staying together. Even today, Palestinian bombers carry out destructive activities in the city. They repeatedly attempt to assert control over the city or avenge the treatment they receive from their Jewish neighbors. Yet, Jerusalem remains part of Israel.

Within Jerusalem, Daniel mentions that the

temple will be defiled. For that to happen, it had to first be rebuilt. Well, the temple in Jerusalem was rebuilt after the prophecy of Daniel and was in use until the Romans destroyed it around A.D. 70. If Daniel's prophecy also applies to the Second Coming, then the temple will be rebuilt again. I believe this will occur around the start of the tribulation period, perhaps in the first few years of the period. Then it will be defiled by the Antichrist when he rises to power in the tribulation period!

Other Old Testament signs remain. They are the numerous references to the events near or during the seven-year tribulation period that immediately precedes the Second Coming. Like the Book of Revelation and the Book of Daniel, many of these writings are full of symbolism. I will refer to a few later when I discuss the tribulation period.

For further reading on the subject of the tribulation period, the following Old Testament books are worth studying:

- Isaiah
- Jeremiah
- Lamentations
- Ezekiel
- Daniel
- Hosea
- Joel
- Amos
- Obadiah
- Jonah
- Micah
- Nahum
- Habakkuk
- Zephaniah
- Haggai
- Zechariah
- Malachi

THE ACCURACY OF BIBLE PROPHESY

I remain amazed at the accuracy of the prophecies God has given us from several thousand years ago. He has a plan for the Second Coming. I hope that as you consider all this material you will be able to see the signs He has given that point to that great event for all who believe in Christ. It is also a little scary that many of the signs have occurred and those that remain will occur over a relatively short period of time.

3

The Coming

Scott, you asked from where Jesus will come and whom will He bring when He comes. This is similar to Karen's concern about how Jesus will come again. You both may be surprised to know how consistent the Bible is in describing what happens at the time of the Second Coming.

The Second Coming of Jesus Christ is a glorious event described in numerous places in the Bible. It will be a spectacular event seen by virtually everyone on earth. Just imagine billions of people throughout the world looking to the sky and seeing the most glorious appearance imaginable.

Although on a much larger scale, the appearance will be similar to Jesus' ascension into heaven when all eleven disciples watched the event. The Book of Acts covers the ascension and foretells of Jesus' return:

> ...he was taken up before their eyes, and a cloud hid him from their sight. They were looking intently up into the sky when suddenly two men

dressed in white stood beside them. "Men of Galilee," they said, "why do you stand here looking into the sky? This same Jesus, who has been taken from you into heaven, will come back in the same way you have seen him go into heaven."

—ACTS 1:9–11

We know that Jesus will return as He left. The disciples watched Him as He ascended in His resurrected body. Likewise, we can expect to see Him descend to earth in similar fashion. The Second Coming will occur at the end of the seven-year tribulation. Jesus will come to bring His kingdom to earth, at the point where those remaining are on the verge of total annihilation. Only by His appearance is the world spared total destruction.

I do not want to dwell on the tribulation here as it is but a backdrop to the return of Jesus. In and of itself, the return will be a display of heavenly power brought to earth. I think you will be impressed by what else is written of the event in the Bible.

In the previous chapter when I discussed the signs of the Second Coming I emphasized Jesus' own words in Matthew 24. Again, in verse 27 He says:

For as lightning that comes from the east is visible even in the west, so will be the coming of the Son of Man.

—MATTHEW 24:27

Jesus goes on to describe the event:

30

Immediately after the distress of those days "the sun will be darkened, and the moon will not give its light; the stars will fall from the sky, and the heavenly bodies will be shaken." At that time the sign of the Son of Man will appear in the sky, and all the nations of the earth will mourn. They will see the Son of Man coming on the clouds of the sky, with power and great glory. And he will send his angels with a loud trumpet call, and they will gather his elect from the four winds, from one end of the heavens to the other.

—MATTHEW 24:29–31

THE DISTRESS OF THOSE DAYS

Jesus' reference to the distress of those days relates to the terrible things happening during the tribulation. But even after those days the attention of the world will be drawn to the fact that the heavens are changing. Light will disappear from the sky and the heavenly bodies will fall, bringing total darkness. Then the sign of our Lord will appear to those who look upon it. Immediately, everyone will realize they are facing the Lord who will judge all, and they will mourn. The Lord will not be alone in the sky. He will call the angels and His elected church to join Him in this glorious appearance.

Luke confirms the description appearing in a dramatic light. Jesus is quoted:

For the Son of Man in his day will be like the lightening, which flashes and lights up the sky from one end to the other.

—LUKE 17:24

31

Jesus sets the stage as to what must happen first before He can return in glory in the verses that follow the one quoted above. He gives us some historical context with which to understand the condition of the world at the time of His coming.

> But first he must suffer many things and be rejected by this generation. Just as it was in the days of Noah, so also will it be in the days of the Son of Man. People were eating, drinking, marrying and being given in marriage up to the day Noah entered the Ark. Then the flood came and destroyed them all. It was the same in the days of Lot. People were eating and drinking, buying and selling, planting and building. But the day Lot left Sodom, fire and sulfur rained down from heaven and destroyed them all.
>
> —LUKE 17:25–29

The context of this event is important. God is bringing judgment at times when it is unexpected. People at the times of Noah and Lot were largely unaware that the wrath that God was about to be waged on them. Therefore, we can expect the tribulation period leading to the Second Coming to commence at a time when most least expect it.

Recently, on September 11, 2001, the entire world was shocked by the sudden terrorist attacks on America. The events caught us by surprise and showed just how complacent we had become. When times are relatively good, we often take things for granted that simply should not be taken for granted.

As the world works through this latest threat of terrorism, we may again find ourselves in a state of prosperity, security and complacency. In such a time, the tribulation God promises may commence.

In Mark, Jesus acknowledges that He is the Son of Man, "and you will see the Son of Man sitting at the right hand of the Mighty One and coming on the clouds of heaven" (Mark 14:62).

So, again we are told that Jesus will return in the sky on the clouds. He will also be seen in the presence of God at His right hand, showing His place of authority.

This matches the prophecy of Daniel where he says:

> In my vision at night I looked, and there before me was one like a son of man, coming with the clouds of heaven. He approached the Ancient of Days and was led into his presence. He was given authority, glory and sovereign power: all peoples, nations and men of every language worshiped him. His dominion is an everlasting dominion that will not pass away, and his kingdom is one that will never be destroyed.
>
> —DANIEL 7:13–14

The apostle Peter describes the Second Coming in this way:

> But the day of the Lord will come like a thief. The heavens will disappear with a roar; the elements will be destroyed by fire, and the earth and everything in it will be laid bare.
>
> —2 PETER 3:10

Here we are told that besides the glorious appearance on the clouds, we can expect the coming to be one of power. The Lord will come with a mission to destroy much of the earth.

The Book of Revelation also depicts a very powerful and vengeful return at the end of the tribulation. This event will take place when warring factions are poised to invade Israel and annihilate its people. In chapter 19 John tells us:

> I saw heaven standing open and there before me was a white horse, whose rider is called Faithful and True. With justice he judges and makes war. His eyes are like blazing fire, and on his head are many crowns. He has a name written on him that no one knows but he himself. He is dressed in a robe dipped in blood, and his name is the Word of God. The armies of heaven were following him, riding on white horses and dressed in fine linen, white and clean. Out of his mouth comes a sharp sword with which to strike down the nations. "He will rule them with an iron scepter." He treads the winepress of the fury of the wrath of God Almighty.
>
> —REVELATION 19:11–15

RETURNING IN GLORY

These biblical verses make it clear that Jesus will return in power and glory. He will come suddenly, and He will be seen riding a white horse. He will wear many crowns and be dressed in a robe dipped in blood. He will be prepared for war.

Christ's return will be preceded by a change in

the physical universe. The light of the world will be the "sign of the Son of Man" when the sun, the moon and the stars are darkened.

The Lord's army will follow Him, and He will take control of the earth quickly bringing His judgment with Him, a judgment that He will dispense swiftly.

THE SECOND COMING IN THE OLD TESTAMENT

I want to relate some of the Old Testament verses to you so you can place what they say in context to both the first and the Second Coming. The Old Testament has many references to the coming of the Messiah, as I have noted earlier. Clearly, prophets like Micah from times as early as 700 B.C. predicted Jesus' first coming. In chapter 5 Micah tells us:

> Marshall your troops, O city of troops, for a siege is laid against us. They will strike Israel's ruler on the cheek with a rod. But you, Bethlehem Ephrathah, though you are small among the clans of Judah, out of you will come for me one who will be ruler over Israel, whose origins are from of old, from ancient times.
>
> —MICAH 5:1–2

This passage helped confirm that Israel's ruler would ultimately come from Bethlehem. This passage has always lent credence to Christ's prophetic birth.

Isaiah tells us:

35

> Hear now, you house of David! Is it not enough to try the patience of men? Will you try the patience of my God also? Therefore the Lord himself will give you a sign: The virgin will be with child and will give birth to a son, and will call him Immanuel.
>
> —Isaiah 7:13–14

Here again the birth of Christ was prophesied. His life was announced hundreds of years before He arrived. He came and fulfilled the prophecy!

Zechariah wrote about the Second Coming around 500 B.C. Many Jews believed that his description of this event would be fulfilled in the first coming of Christ. The powerful appearance depicted in the book of Revelation in the New Testament is the same power Zechariah said would occur when the Lord comes. He says:

> A day of the LORD is coming when your plunder will be divided among you. I will gather all the nations to Jerusalem to fight against it: the city will be captured, the houses ransacked, and the women raped. Half the city will go into exile, but the rest of the people will not be taken from the city.
>
> Then the LORD will go out and fight against those nations, as he fights in the day of battle. On that day his feet will stand on the Mount of Olives, east of Jerusalem, and the Mount of Olives will be split in two from east to west, forming a great valley, with half of the mountain moving north and half moving south. You will flee my mountain valley, for it will extend to Azel. You will flee as you fled from the earthquake in the days of Uzziah king of Judah. Then the LORD my

God will come, and all the holy ones with him.

On that day there will be no light, no cold or frost. It will be a unique day, without daytime or nighttime—a day known to the LORD. When evening comes there will be light. On that day living water will flow out from Jerusalem, half to the eastern sea and half to the western sea, in summer and in winter. The LORD will be king over the whole earth. On that day there will be one LORD, and his name the only name.

—ZECHARIAH 14:1–9

Not knowing this was a description of the Second Coming, I can see how many of the Jews expected these events to take place when the Lord first appeared. Jesus confused them with His grace and mercy. Even His miracles did not convince these leaders who expected a "Zechariah-type" of appearance.

Interestingly, Zechariah tells us of the "holy ones" the Lord will bring with Him. He does not tell us who these holy ones are, but other biblical verses reveal more about those who will accompany the Lord at His return.

ARMIES OF HEAVEN

Revelation 19, as noted above, tells us that "armies of heaven were following him, riding on white horses and dressed in fine linen." We learn what they will be doing and how they will be dressed, but not who they are.

Jesus alludes to the gathering of help to accompany His return. In Matthew, Mark and Luke He is quoted as saying He will draw together this help. In Mark He puts it: "And he will send his angels and gather his elect from the four winds, from the ends of the earth to the ends of the heavens" (Mark 13:27).

In the Book of Jude, we are told that Enoch, the seventh from Adam, prophesied about these men. He said, "See, the Lord is coming with thousands upon thousands of his holy ones to judge everyone, and to convict all the ungodly of all the ungodly acts they have done in the ungodly way, and of all the harsh words ungodly sinners have spoken against him" (Jude 14–15).

I believe the holy ones and the elect refer to the angels and the resurrected souls Christ brings to heaven before His Second Coming. I describe these resurrected souls in the chapter on heaven-bound souls.

At any rate, we know He will come in glory from heaven and He will come in force to establish His kingdom on earth. He will bring help and He will be victorious in every way imaginable. This glorious and powerful event ends the seven-year tribulation and brings His kingdom to earth. Jesus will rule!

4

FOR WHOM
HE COMES

Karen wants to know, "Who will be chosen to be with Jesus?" Likewise, Scott wants to know, "For whom will Jesus come?"

These questions are very similar. In answering them, I want to relate a little history that I think will help. Then I will answer Karen's question. It answers a lot of Scott's question, but I will need to expand on the answer to Scott's question because his involves not only those chosen, but it includes those who are not chosen as well.

Actually, a lot is written on this subject because it gets at the fundamental reason for Jesus' coming. Thanks for asking the questions the way you did, because in all honesty I had never framed my thoughts much beyond whether Jesus would come for us or not. Your questions forced a broader look.

Historically speaking, Jewish history is a good starting point because it is there that we get a better idea of God's overall plan. The Jewish people have considered themselves to be God's chosen people for thousands of years with good reason. God told Abraham just over four thousand years ago to sacrifice his son Isaac to show his allegiance to God. Although God stopped Abraham from following through with the sacrifice, He knew Abraham would obey God. God blessed Abraham and made a lasting covenant with him and with the Hebrew people. Having promised to Noah in earlier days that He would not again destroy the population of the earth, God went on to promise many descendants from Abraham and that those descendants would occupy the land of Israel.

As the Hebrew descendants of Abraham multiplied, the Jewish faith emerged. Moses brought the commandments to the Hebrew people. Prophets foretold of events that increased hope for prosperity and salvation. Yet, the Hebrew people turned against God many times, and God punished them with wars and long periods of exile.

Throughout all this time, one of the major hopes held by the Jewish people was for the glorious appearing of the Messiah as promised in Scripture. Messiah would lead them to a final victory over evil and allow them to reign forever in peace and prosperity. They have continued to wait for thousands of years. When Jesus came to the Hebrew people they rejected Him, and this led to their being condemned. In Luke, Jesus says:

> The days will come upon you when your enemies will build an embankment against you and encircle you and hem you in on every side. They

will dash you to the ground, you and the children
within your walls. They will not leave one stone
on another, because you did not recognize the
time of God's coming to you.

—LUKE 19:43–44

It was not long before Jesus' prophetic word
came to pass. The Romans destroyed the city in
A.D. 70. Still the Jewish people failed to accept
Jesus as the Son of God.

Jesus came in love and humility to bear witness
to the truth, fulfill the Scriptures, die for sin and be
resurrected. He did all this so that we who believe
would have eternal life.

In doing all that He did, Jesus opened a time for
the church of non-Jewish people to accept His
Word, repent of sin, bear witness to His resurrection and grow in love and faith through worship
and the doing of good works throughout the
world. Billions of Christians have emerged from
that opening, and all of us have been given the
chance to realize eternal salvation through God's
hope and Jesus' resurrection. What a blessing!

Believers in Christ will be saved. All who have
died since the church began and who turned to
Jesus before their death will be saved. All who live
in Christ at the time of His coming will be saved.
All who stand by Jesus during the tribulation will
be saved. The Lord's mercy is great!

In Jesus' first coming it was clear from the beginning that He came to save sinners. The Scriptures
tell us of an angel's pronouncement to Joseph

before Mary gave birth to Jesus:

> She will give birth to a son, and you will give him the name Jesus, because he will save his people from their sins.
>
> —MATTHEW 1:21

With great mercy God brought Jesus into the world to save sinners. This was Jesus' first coming. In John, Jesus says:

> For God so loved the world that he gave his one and only Son, that whoever believes in him shall not perish but have eternal life. For God did not send his Son into the world to condemn the world, but to save the world through him. Whoever believes in him is not condemned, but whoever does not believe stands condemned already because he has not believed in the name of God's one and only Son.
>
> —JOHN 3:16–18

Likewise, it is clear that in His Second Coming, Jesus is coming first for believers! The emphasis on one's belief in Jesus is paramount to God. Believing in Jesus is not just one way to salvation. It is clearly the only way.

I have known many people who are convinced that if they live a righteous life, as they define it, they have as good a chance of being saved as anyone who believes in Jesus. They cite the many religions of the world that venerate good virtues and believe in a gracious God.

Yet, the above passage from the Gospel of John

makes it clear that in the end, belief in Jesus is essential to receiving salvation. The Lord's sacrifice for our sins is the key that opens the door for salvation. A failure to recognize Jesus as the Son of God is a failure to recognize God.

Jesus confirmed the essential nature of belief in Him in the following quote taken from John:

> I am the bread of life. He who comes to me will never go hungry, and he who believes in me will never be thirsty. But as I told you, you have seen me and still do not believe. All that the father gives me will come to me, and whoever comes to me I will never drive away. For I have come down from heaven not to do my will but to do the will of him who sent me. And this is the will of him who sent me, that I shall lose none of all that he has given me, but raise them up at the last day. For my Father's will is that everyone who looks to the Son and believes in him shall have eternal life, and I will raise him up at the last day.
>
> —JOHN 6:35–40

Clearly, Jesus was sent to us on a mission from God the Father. He came to bring salvation to those who turn to Jesus and believe in Him. That salvation involves raising all believers, whether dead or alive, to heaven above at the end of time. It is about that simple for believers!

Keep in mind what Jesus tells us:

> I am the way and the truth and the life. No one comes to the Father except through me.
>
> —JOHN 14:6

In this message of salvation, we understand the responsibility God entrusted to Jesus. It could not be clearer to anyone who sees the truth. If you are interested in eternal life, then you must believe in Jesus as the Son of God. He brought us the truth, and it is only through His life and sacrifice that we live with the promise of salvation.

So, Karen, the answer to your question on who will be chosen to be with Jesus is right here in Scripture. Believers in Jesus will be chosen!

Scott's question is partially answered at this point. We know Jesus is coming for believers, but what about everyone else?

The Scriptures are clear in answering this question also. Jesus is coming to judge everyone. I will discuss the subject of judgment in chapter eight as it relates to the actions taken by Jesus at His Second Coming. Here I simply want to emphasize that Jesus is coming for everyone on earth in one form or another. He has been charged by God to judge the world. So He will bring swift judgment, by all accounts, when He comes. In the Book of John Jesus explains this role:

> Moreover, the Father judges no one, but has entrusted all judgment to the Son, that all may honor the Son just as they honor the Father. He who does not honor the Son does not honor the Father, who sent him.
>
> I tell you the truth, whoever hears my word and believes him who sent me has eternal life and will not be condemned; he has crossed over from death to life. I tell you the truth, a time is coming and has

now come when the dead will hear the voice of the
Son of God and those who hear will live. For as the
Father has life in himself, so he has granted the Son
to have life in himself. And he has given him
authority to judge because he is the Son of Man.

Do not be amazed at this, for a time is coming
when all who are in their graves will hear his voice
and come out—those who have done good will
rise to live, and those who have done evil will rise
to be condemned. By myself I can do nothing; I
judge only as I hear, and my judgment is just, for I
seek not to please myself but him who sent me.

—JOHN 5:22–30

Again, Jesus' role as judge is underscored in
Matthew when He tells us that judgment will lead
to rewards for those who do the will of God:

For the Son of Man is going to come in his
Father's glory with his angels, and then he will
reward each person according to what he has
done.

—MATTHEW 16:27

I know many people wonder about the difference in contributions made by individual
Christians. They wonder if those differences determine whether they will be saved or whether they
will receive recognition for their contributions.
Hence, an important concept to keep in mind is
that gaining eternal life is based on one's belief in
Jesus, whereas obtaining rewards is based on what
one does.

The concept of reward is also mentioned in the
Book of Revelation where Jesus tells John:

Behold, I am coming soon! My reward is with me, and I will give to everyone according to what he has done. I am the Alpha and the Omega, the First and the Last, the Beginning and the End.

—REVELATION 22:12–13

Both judgment and reward can be expected at the Second Coming. Using His judgment, Jesus will separate the good from the bad. When Jesus comes He will separate everyone for the sake of judgment. This is not conjecture. This is the truth!

As you read through some of the scriptures noted in chapter eight, you will see that Jesus made it crystal clear that His judgment involves separation of those who believe and those who do not. Rewards will be given to the believers, and condemnation will be given to the nonbelievers.

Again, if we are prepared for Jesus and believe in Him, He will receive us. Those who are not prepared will be condemned. And with so much written in the Bible on this subject, it is evident that this subject was vitally important to the disciples. Likewise, Jesus and the disciples realized how important it would be for future followers.

To prepare for eternal life, Jesus expects us to believe in Him and in His Word. This is not solely His desire alone, but it is also the desire of God.

BELIEF AND GOOD WORKS

Preparation goes beyond belief, as Jesus fully expects us to put into practice our belief through the doing of good works. These works manifest themselves in the godly virtues that I will discuss in-depth in the next chapter.

Before moving on to the preparation questions I got from three of you, I want to mention the rapture. The rapture has to do, in part, with the question, For whom is Jesus coming? I believe the Bible tells us that Jesus will come for Christians before the judgment of the world takes place.

I will discuss the rapture at some length in chapter seven in answer to questions from Deidre. There I will relate what I believe the Bible tells about the timing of the rapture and what happens during the rapture. But here I want to briefly address the rapture because it will be a huge event in the course of human history.

I want you to keep in mind that for over two thousand years God worked with the Hebrew people to get them to live in obedience to His will. When He finally sent Jesus, the Hebrew people and particularly the Hebrew leaders rejected Him. The body of Christ, or His church, has grown over the last two thousand years based on His life, His teachings, His Word, His sacrifice, His resurrection, the Holy Spirit and the lives of countless saints and righteous individuals who carried the gospel into the world.

As the time of the great tribulation nears, God does not intend for all of the believers in Christ to suffer the devastation that comes with this period. Just as God removed Noah and Lot from impending disaster, I believe God will remove the true believers before the tribulation. Therefore, since the entire earth is to suffer the tribulation, then the rapture must remove true believers from the earth.

The basis for this belief and a description of who is chosen comes to us in Paul's first letter to the Thessalonians. He tells us:

> Brothers, we do not want to be ignorant about those who fall asleep, or to grieve like the rest of men, who have no hope. We believe that Jesus died and rose again and so we believe that God will bring with Jesus those who have fallen asleep in him. According to the Lord's own word, we tell you that we who are still alive, who are left to the coming of the Lord, will certainly not precede those who have fallen asleep. For the Lord himself will come down from heaven, with a loud command, with the voice of the archangel and with the trumpet call of God, and the dead in Christ will rise first. After that, we who are still alive will be caught up together with them in the clouds to meet the Lord in the air. And so we will be with the Lord forever.
>
> —1 THESSALONIANS 4:13–17

Here Paul is trying to provide reassurance to members of the church that those who have died in Christ will be saved. He comforts them with the thought that God will bring them to Christ. Those who are alive at the time of Jesus' Second Coming can expect to join Christ after He has called those who have died. Together all these souls will meet Jesus in the air.

Likewise in Revelation, the Lord says to the faithful at the church of Philadelphia:

> Since you have kept my command to endure patiently, I will also keep you from the hour of trial that is going to come upon the whole world to test those who live on the earth.
>
> —REVELATION 3:10

Paired with Paul's preceding message, we understand that this gathering of the faithful in Christ will occur before the trial during the tribulation. Since Jesus will not have made His Second Coming at the end of the tribulation, the faithful in Christ will have to go to Him in the air. In other words, these saints will experience a form of resurrection.

Paul helps us understand who is with Christ and who is chosen by Him. In his first letter to the Corinthians he describes what life is like in Christ for those who really believe and live in holiness. Paul says:

> Since, then, you have been raised with Christ, set your hearts on things above, where Christ is seated at the right hand of God. Set your mind on things above, not on earthly things. For you died, and your life is now hidden with Christ in God. When Christ, who is your life, appears, then you also will appear with him in glory.
>
> Put to death, therefore, whatever belongs to your earthly nature: sexual mortality, impurity, lust, evil desires and greed, which is idolatry. Because of these, the wrath of God is coming. You used to walk in these ways, in the life you once lived. But now you must rid yourselves of all such

things as these: anger, rage, malice, slander, and filthy language from your lips. Do not lie to each other, since you have taken off your old self with its practices and have put on the new self, which is being renewed in knowledge in the image of its Creator. Here there is no Greek or Jew, circumcised or uncircumcised, barbarian, Scythian, slave or free, but Christ is all, and is in all.

Therefore, as God's chosen people, holy and dearly loved, clothe yourselves with compassion, gentleness and patience. Bear with each other and forgive whatever grievances you may have against one another. Forgive as the Lord forgave you. And over all these virtues put love, which binds them all together in perfect unity. Let the peace of Christ rule in your hearts, since as members of one body you were called to peace.

—COLOSSIANS 3:1–15

Therefore, faith in Jesus is essential to being chosen. We must be believers! Next, manifesting that faith in what we say and do is expected and required of Jesus. The chapter that follows addresses an important question from Scott on preparation, and it helps us see the virtues we must strive to have to serve Christ. I hope you grow in understanding and manifesting your faith in Christ!

5

PREPARATION

Three of your questions fall into the category I consider as "preparation." Karen asked, "What do I have to do in my life to be chosen?" Ken asked, "What does one need to do to prepare for this event?" Scott asked, "What virtues do we need to be saved?" This chapter on preparation represents the most relevant and important topic of all.

What makes the preparation so relevant and important is that it is totally within our power to be prepared. We control all that is necessary to be prepared, and we have no one to blame but ourselves if we are not.

To be chosen one needs to believe in Jesus as the Son of God. As I mentioned in the preceding chapter, God demands that we believe in Jesus, who came from heaven to earth to save us. It is through Him that we are saved.

Believing in Jesus Christ requires more than lip service or simply saying that we believe. The Bible suggests that our faith requires good works as an outward expression of our inward belief, because God is looking for real evidence of our faith. So it is incumbent upon us to use our gifts, not only to worship God, but also to help others with their needs. In doing so, we follow Jesus' example and do the will of the Father.

LIVING BY THE COMMANDMENTS

The Old Testament version of being prepared meant living by the commandments of God. Jesus, when asked which commandments were most important, replied:

> "Love the Lord your God with all your heart and with all your soul and with all your mind and with all your strength." The second is this: "Love your neighbor as yourself." There is no commandment greater than these.
>
> —MARK 12:30–31

Jesus continued to teach us about life and the virtues we should strive to possess in preparing for the kingdom of God. But everything He said was built upon the fundamentals outlined in the Old Testament Law. In the New Testament, His Word presents a deeper understanding of the personal virtues He expects of His followers. I want to share with you a summary of what Jesus taught about these virtues. Perhaps this lengthy answer will help you grow into the Christian you are capable of becoming.

WHY VIRTUES?

In times past, I would stop to reflect about the person I would like to be and think about how others see me. I would get overwhelmed with who I was and where I was in terms of personal growth. It seemed too far to travel from where I was at a given point of time and where I wanted to be. My view of the future lacked substance, which caused me to sometimes submit to letting others dictate who I would become instead of taking the initiative to become the man I wanted to be. I would just go with the flow sometimes and not really do what I wanted to do. I think we all are guilty of this in varying degrees.

Bombarded by advertising and popular trends, it becomes too easy to find ourselves driven by the expectations of others and molded into someone else's image of what we should be. We all must work at not letting the appeal of television commercials motivate us *en masse* toward their own agendas for our lives. Popular movements are temporary and can be consuming campaigns designed to motivate us in ways that may or may not be good for us. Again, we need to focus on the future with moral substance in mind. We must continually remind ourselves that we are in control and that we can and should exercise control, or we will suffer by being misled.

Personal Beliefs and Principles

As I look at today's world of rapid information transfer, I see the pace of life accelerating for most people. This increasing pace increases our involvement in worldly events, and it makes us vulnerable to the trendy movements all around us. In such a world, it is vital to build our lives on a firm foundation of beliefs and principles.

Beliefs and the principles that direct those beliefs into action are the source of our actions. If we do not believe in anything, we become vulnerable to being led into many different directions at the drop of a hat.

Christian beliefs are based upon our allegiance to God the Father, God the Son and God the Holy Spirit. Likewise, as Christians our commitment to others is second only to our commitment to God. These beliefs become the substance in our lives.

Christ knew that we would need direction to manifest our beliefs through our actions. While the Old Testament gave us the principles or commandments that we need to follow in our lives, Jesus went further by teaching us key virtues that should be evident in us as we build upon His system of beliefs and commandments. His Word helps us to understand what things we need to do to truly be believers. We are all a work-in-progress!

Aspiring to a virtuous life with Christ requires us to identify our individual gifts and then put those gifts to work for Him. Doing this helps us grow in a direction consistent with our beliefs while we sort through all the stress and activity of modern life.

Let me be clear about what I mean when I say *virtues*. Virtues are those characteristics that form goodness, worthiness and purity in one's life. They are the admirable traits that represent quality in one's existence and help define who we really are. They may be gifted to us by God or developed through perseverance. They are good, not evil, by their very nature. These godly traits are available to all of us if we choose to pursue them.

If virtues are important, what are the virtues to which we should aspire? Who says they are important? Can we really understand them? Can we do anything about changing ourselves to acquire these virtues? These are questions I want to answer for you to help you understand how you can use your gifts to prepare for the Second Coming.

Many books and articles have been written on virtues. Many organizations share virtues to which their members aspire. Most are good and well meaning, but some can be self-serving, lacking in true authority and confusing. Therefore, we must search the Word of Christ Jesus to find His direction regarding virtues. Therein, we can be certain of the authority, direction and clarity spoken in truth with an absolute connection to our beliefs as Christians.

Throughout the first four Gospels of the New Testament, Jesus illuminates key virtues as being important. After noting these many references, I found common themes running through them. Grouping them became somewhat arbitrary, but seven virtues stood out in this process. Generally speaking, these seven include all the virtues professed by Christ. Furthermore, the seven are as relevant to life today as they were when the Scriptures were first written.

The seven virtues discussed in this chapter are presented as a means to facilitate our understanding of the Word of God. The categories are simply a way of helping me understand what I need to concentrate on as I strive to fulfill our Christian beliefs. I hope they do the same for you.

What follows is a discussion of virtues with quotes from Jesus as written in the first four Gospels of the New Testament. It is written to promote thought and emphasize relevance to everyday life. Hopefully, an enhanced understanding of Christ's messages on virtues will help focus our gifts and energy on being better Christians. Hopefully too it will strengthen our Christian obligation to become examples to others who may join us in our journey with Christ.

AUTHORITY IN WHAT CHRIST SAYS

Before any of us can understand and commit to the virtues professed by Christ, we must recognize His authority. After all, it is His life, His sacrifice and His promise of salvation that draw us to His Word. His authority is the basis for our Christian beliefs.

My most fundamental belief in life is in the

existence of a righteous and merciful God who through the sacrifice and resurrection of His Son provided everyone a means to obtain forgiveness of sin and eternal life. Following Jesus' baptism by John the Baptist, Matthew's Gospel notes:

> As soon as Jesus was baptized, he went up out of the water. At that moment heaven was opened, and he saw the Spirit of God descending like a dove and lighting on him. And a voice from heaven said, "This is my Son, whom I love; with him I am well pleased."
>
> —MATTHEW 3:16–17

This same story is retold in the Gospel of Mark and Luke, confirming that John the Baptist preceded Jesus' arrival and announced His presence and authority. God confirmed this authority in the presence of many witnesses.

Again, at a time when Peter, James and James' brother John accompanied Jesus to a mountaintop where they witnessed Jesus' transfiguration, God said:

> This is my Son, whom I love; with him I am well pleased. Listen to him!
>
> —MATTHEW 17:5

These disciples heard God's own words declaring Jesus' authority. Jesus accepted that authority, and He acknowledges His authority in a number of passages in the New Testament. In Matthew He says:

> Whoever acknowledges me before men, I will also

acknowledge him before my Father in heaven. But whoever disowns me before men, I will disown him before my Father in heaven.

—MATTHEW 10:32–33

This important passage from Jesus not only affirms His recognition of the authority God placed in Him, but it tells us that He will serve as the intermediary for God and all people on earth. It also reveals that Jesus will either acknowledge or disown us before the Father based upon our belief in Him.

Later in Matthew He tells us:

All authority in heaven and on earth has been given to me. Therefore go and make disciples of all nations, baptizing them in the name of the Father and of the Son and of the Holy Spirit, and teaching them to obey everything I have commanded you. And surely I am with you always, to the very end of the age.

—MATTHEW 28:18–20

Here Jesus confirms His authority. He makes His charge to His disciples clear that baptizing and teaching are expected.

In John Jesus tells us:

For God so loved the world that he gave his one and only Son, that whoever believes in him shall not perish but have eternal life. For God did not send his Son into the world to condemn the world, but to save the world through him.

—JOHN 3:16–17

This passage indicates that Jesus is the only Son of God who shows us the way to eternal life. We need not fear that God intends to condemn us, but instead He seeks our salvation through His Son.

Jesus had many things to teach us during His time with us. He wanted us to gain understanding so we would deepen our faith in the same way that He had learned from God. Essentially, He sought to bring God's will closer to us so we could hear it, teach it and know it. In John He says:

> My teaching is not my own. It comes from him who sent me.
>
> —JOHN 7:16

In this verse, Jesus acknowledges the authority of God and the fact that He is representing the will of God. He knows He must do His part to carry out God's will, and He must take what has been given to Him and extend it to us. He says:

> I am the bread of life. He who comes to me will never go hungry, and he who believes in me will never be thirsty.
>
> —JOHN 6:35

To those who believe in Him, He says:

> If you hold to my teaching, you are really my disciples. Then you will know the truth, and the truth will set you free.
>
> —JOHN 8:31–32

Jesus makes it clear to us that He is sent to us by God. He came on no other authority. He said:

...for I came from God and now am here. I have not come on my own; but he sent me.

—JOHN 8:42

This purpose is also echoed when He says:

... I am the light of the world. Whoever follows me will never walk in darkness, but will have the light of life.

—JOHN 8:12

LIGHT AND DARKNESS

Repeatedly the Bible carefully distinguishes between light and darkness. Light is associated with God, and darkness is associated with evil. God brought light into the world during creation in the literal sense, and God brings a personal and spiritual light into the world through Jesus. Yet, Jesus makes it clear that a direct connection with God exists, as noted in John where he says:

When a man believes in me, he does not believe in me only, but in the one who sent me. When he looks at me, he sees the one who sent me. I have come into the world as a light, so that no one who believes in me should stay in darkness.

—JOHN 12:44–46

This distinction between light and darkness helps us to gain a clearer understanding of Jesus. When we are frustrated or in anguish over something, we feel as if we are in darkness. When we do something evil, we feel as if we are in darkness. On the other hand, when we feel good about something, we feel that we are surrounded by light. So Jesus is here to bring light into our lives and to show us a way out of the darkness.

Jesus' promise to us extends to our life hereafter. He makes it clear that He is the very key to eternal life. At the time Jesus goes to Bethany and raises Lazarus from the dead He proclaims in John:

> I am the resurrection and the life. He who believes in me will live, even though he dies; and whoever lives and believes in me will never die.
>
> —JOHN 11:25–26

Jesus' message of eternal life is a promise to all people. He did not single out anyone who believes in Him. It is a promise of inclusion!

Although He was crucified, Jesus steadfastly carried out His sacrifice for us. God was prepared to endure this sacrifice in a manner similar to what Abraham was prepared to do with his son Isaac. Jesus knew He must die to complete this sacrifice and to give all believers a chance for redemption through Him. Even so, He certainly realized that He had power to change the events at His crucifixion, for in Matthew He says:

> Do you think I cannot call on my Father, and he will at once put at my disposal more than twelve legions of angels? But how then would the Scriptures be fulfilled that say it must happen this way?
>
> —MATTHEW 26:53–54

Jesus held to the Scriptures that reflected the will

of God. He could have called upon tens of thousands of angels to rescue Him. He could have changed the course of history, but that would not have been consistent with the Scriptures.

Jesus' authority is clear. It comes from God, and we should view His teachings as being from God. Paired with a promise of salvation, these teachings represent the preeminent truth in the world. Jesus provided us with a full and perfect insight into God's will for us. He shared this insight throughout the Gospels where His messages can be read and understood. So let us learn from Jesus' words and do good works with them to add to the glory of God.

OBEDIENCE

Although Jesus brought a new covenant from God and paid for that covenant with His life, He did so in a manner consistent with the Word of God. In His obedience to God He restored the covenant relationship for our sake.

When Jesus reached the Jordan River where John the Baptist was baptizing and preaching about coming Messiah, John was reluctant to baptize Jesus. Yet, John did baptize Him because Jesus instructed him to do so.

Following Jesus' baptism and several years of teachings, He prepared the disciples for His departure by instructing them to obey what He had commanded:

> Whoever has my commands and obeys them, he is

the one who loves me. He who loves me will be loved by my Father, and I too will love him and show myself to him.

—JOHN 14:21

Here Jesus ties obedience to love. Again He expects that belief in Him must be demonstrated through righteous actions. These statements ring consistent with His early teachings in which He said:

For I tell you that unless your righteousness surpasses that of the Pharisees and the teachers of the law, you will certainly not enter the kingdom of heaven.

—MATTHEW 5:20

Likewise, Jesus made it clear in Luke that the Law and the prophets of the Old Testament were being fulfilled by Him, and they would remain relevant for the future. "The Law" refers to the first five books of the Old Testament. "The prophets" refers to the major, minor and other prophetic books of the Old Testament. In Luke Christ says:

The Law and the Prophets were proclaimed until John. Since that time, the good news of the kingdom of God is being preached, and everyone is forcing his way into it. It is easier for heaven and earth to disappear than for the least stroke of a pen to drop out of the Law.

—LUKE 16:16–17

Jesus did not want us to ignore the past commandments and simply rely on His forgiveness with a promise of salvation. He fully expects us to obey the commandments and learn to live with the spirit they embody as well as the authority they carry.

As to the commandments, Jesus was asked which was most important. He answered this question directly, and He points to the key messages of the Ten Commandments in His answer recorded in Mark:

> "The most important one," answered Jesus, "is this: 'Hear, O Israel, the Lord our God, the Lord is one. Love the Lord your God with all your heart and with all your soul and with all your mind and with all your strength.' The second is this: 'Love your neighbor as yourself.' There is no commandment greater than these."
>
> —MARK 12:29–31

For over a thousand years the Ten Commandments Moses delivered to the Hebrews served as God's expectation in the covenant between God and the Hebrew people. Moses lived approximately fourteen hundred years before Christ, and in the Book of Exodus, Moses recites the commandments from God. Jesus affirmed that they apply to today and the future. He focused our attention on loving God and our neighbors.

Jesus wanted us to strive to live by these commandments. Our position in heaven will be based, in part, upon our efforts to comply with the Law and how we influence others to do the same.

The commandments of the Old Testament are part of the covenant relationship God has with us. God made a covenant with Noah to never destroy the population of the world again. He made one with Abraham promising faithfulness to Abraham and his descendants. He made one with Moses and the Hebrews promising protection and land. Finally, through the life of His Son Jesus Christ, He made one with all who repent of their sins and believe in Christ as Savior. He offers eternal life!

These covenant or promise relationships with God are what God asks in return. He asks that we might be faithful to Him in living a righteous life. That is why He gives us the commandments and the Word of Christ. We should be able to understand what is expected of us and what is important to God. Furthermore, we should be able to grow as individuals and to do our work following the spirit of God's will.

Importantly, God knew it would be difficult for us as believers to avoid evil temptations in our lives. Therefore, simply providing His commandments was not enough. Likewise, the example set by Jesus in His life and the Word He gave needed spiritual reinforcement to counter the evil forces at work in the world. As a result, Jesus tells His disciples of the coming of the Holy Spirit:

> If you love me, you will obey what I command. And I will ask the Father, and he will give you another Counselor to be with you forever—the Spirit of Truth.
>
> —JOHN 14:15–17

He goes on to say:

> All this I have spoken while still with you. But the
> Counselor, the Holy Spirit, whom the Father will
> send in my name, will teach you all things and
> remind you of everything I have said to you.
>
> —JOHN 14:25–26

As our conscience works to remind us of what is good, we are blessed as believers in Christ to have the Holy Spirit to help us. As we hear the gospel preached, we are blessed to have the Holy Spirit help us understand it. We can rely on this spiritual reinforcement in prayer and in daily life.

With the spiritual reinforcement of the Holy Spirit, we should strive to understand Jesus' teachings on the commandments so we can better follow them. An important teaching on this subject was delivered to crowds of followers near the Sea of Galilee. His remarks aimed at the commandments are found in Matthew 5 and 6.

These teachings reflect Jesus' desire for an expanded understanding of the commandments. He widens the interpretation of these commandments and gets at the spirit they cast as well as the specific meaning. Although He does not address each of the commandments, He gives enough examples of how we can better deal with all of them. I suggest you read these two chapters.

In His desire to see us live an obedient life, Jesus gives us some advice about the value we place on God. He says:

No one can serve two masters. Either he will hate the one and love the other, or he will be devoted to the one and despise the other. You cannot serve both God and Money. Therefore, I tell you, do not worry about your life, what you will eat or drink; or about your body, what you will wear. Is not life more important than clothes?

—MATTHEW 6:24–25

This passage tells us that God is concerned about whether we serve him or some other master. God is a jealous god on this issue and will have no gods served with or above Him.

Jesus goes on to tell us where to focus our lives:

But seek first his kingdom and his righteousness, and all these things will be given to you as well. Therefore do not worry about tomorrow, for tomorrow will worry about itself. Each day has enough trouble of its own.

—MATTHEW 6:33–34

What wonderful news! Jesus cuts to the key issue about what should and should not be important in our lives. He realizes that we are tempted constantly, but He wants us to understand what is expected. He keeps the message simple, and He puts our busy day-to-day lives in right relationship to the greater plan God has in mind for us.

In His early teachings, Jesus emphasized the Spirit in what is expected of us. He prefaced His comments on adherence to the Law by outlining for His disciples what are commonly called the Beatitudes. In Matthew He says:

Blessed are the poor in spirit, for theirs is the kingdom of heaven. Blessed are those who mourn, for they will be comforted. Blessed are the meek, for they will inherit the earth. Blessed are those who hunger and thirst for righteousness, for they will be filled. Blessed are the merciful, for they will be shown mercy. Blessed are the pure in heart, for they will see God. Blessed are the peacemakers, for they will be called sons of God. Blessed are those who are persecuted because of righteousness, for theirs is the kingdom of heaven. Blessed are you when people insult you and falsely say all kinds of evil against you because of me. Rejoice and be glad, because great is your reward in heaven, for in the same way they persecuted the prophets who were before you.

—MATTHEW 5:3–12

Jesus shows that He understands all about the failings of mankind and how we have failed to obey the Law. Through His sacrifice He brings reconciliation for our sins. However, He wants us to recognize that there is much more to the Law than a literal interpretation. He wants us to recognize and learn that obeying the Law means fulfilling our covenant responsibility to God. That responsibility includes developing a fellowship with others that meets God's expectations. Those expectations come to us as virtues God deems to be important. The Beatitudes reinforce this expanded expectation in being obedient.

God expects us to believe in His Son. Belief includes a commitment of the spirit and a manifestation of the body and the mind to do the good works of Christ. Likewise, obedience gets to the spirit of doing what is righteous, not just the adherence to the letter of the Law.

Jesus recognized that the Word of God would be received and obeyed differently. The difference is in the depth to which one is able to change from doing his or her own will to doing the will of God. He elaborates with a parable in Luke:

> "A farmer went out to sow his seed. As he was scattering the seed, some fell along the path; it was trampled on, and the birds of the air ate it up. Some fell on rock, and when it came up, the plants withered because they had no moisture. Other seed fell among thorns, which grew up with it and choked the plants. Still other seed fell on good soil. It came up and yielded a crop, a hundred times more than was sown."
>
> When he said this, he called out, "He who has ears to hear, let him hear."
>
> His disciples asked him what the parable meant. He said, "The knowledge of the secrets of the kingdom of God has been given to you, but to others I speak in parables, so that, 'though seeing, they may not see; though hearing, they may not understand.'"
>
> "This is the meaning of the parable: The seed is the word of God. Those along the path are the ones who hear, and then the devil comes and takes away the word from their hearts, so that they may not believe and be saved. Those on the rock are the ones who receive the word with joy when they hear it, but they have no root. They believe for awhile, but in the time of testing they fall away. The seed that fell among the thorns stands for

those who hear, but as they go on their way they are choked by life's worries, riches and pleasures, and they do not mature. But the seed on good soil stands for those with a noble and good heart, who hear the word, retain it, and by persevering produce a crop."

—LUKE 8:5–15

Through Jesus we have a right relationship with God. This new covenant calls us to repent for our sins, accept God's forgiveness, trust in God and live in fellowship with others. This relationship necessitates that we obey His will, and it leads directly into the other virtues highlighted by Jesus.

REPENTANCE

Repentance is a critical virtue in our lives, for we all must recognize our inherent inability to perfect obedience to God. Because of our earlier failings, Jesus came into the world to save sinners. Therefore, we must repent.

So what does it mean to repent? It means to feel truly sorry about the sins we have committed in our lives. Second, it means that we are dedicated to turning away from the wrong and turning to what is right.

Jesus spoke early on in His teachings about the importance of repentance. In Matthew He said:

Repent, for the kingdom of heaven is near.

—MATTHEW 4:17

In Luke we are told:

> But the Pharisees and the teachers of the law who belonged to their sect complained to his disciples, "Why do you eat and drink with tax collectors and 'sinners'?" Jesus answered them, "It is not the healthy who need a doctor, but the sick. I have not come to call the righteous, but sinners to repentance."
>
> —LUKE 5:30–32

Christ Jesus provides us, as sinners, a way of reconciliation. It begins with repentance and ends with great joy in heaven. But repentance is a must as noted in the following from Luke:

> Now there were some present at that time who told Jesus about the Galileans whose blood Pilate had mixed with their sacrifices. Jesus answered, "Do you think that these Galileans were worse sinners because they suffered this way? I tell you, no! But unless you repent, you too will perish. Or those eighteen who died when the tower in Siloam fell on them—do you think they were more guilty than all the others living in Jerusalem? I tell you, no! But unless you repent, you too will all perish."
>
> —LUKE 13:1–5

Therefore, the path to reconciliation begins with repentance. Only those who are in full obedience to God do not need repentance. That leaves out most, if not all, of the people I know! The alternative is clear. Without repentance a person with sin will perish.

Jesus also makes it clear that through repentance we have a chance to return to doing right. Yet if we fail to do right, we will still perish. This is symbolized in Jesus' parable of the fig tree:

A man had a fig tree, planted in his vineyard, and he went to look for fruit on it, but did not find any. So he said to the man who took care of the vineyard, "For three years now I've been coming to look for fruit on this fig tree and haven't found any. Cut it down! Why should it use up the soil?" "Sir," the man replied, "leave it alone for one more year, and I'll dig around it and fertilize it. If it bears fruit next year then fine! If not, then cut it down."

—LUKE 13:6–9

This parable symbolizes God's willingness to give sinners another chance to turn their lives around. However, if they fail to do so they will suffer the fate of death.

Jesus goes on to tell us of the great joy it brings to have a sinner repent. In the parable of the lost sheep Jesus teaches us about conversion:

Now the tax collectors and "sinners" were all gathering around to hear him. But the Pharisees and the teachers of the law muttered, "This man welcomes sinners and eats with them." Then Jesus told them this parable: "Suppose one of you has a hundred sheep and loses one of them. Does he not leave the ninety-nine in the open country and go after the lost sheep until he finds it? And when he finds it, he joyfully puts it on his shoulders and goes home. Then he calls his friends and neighbors together and says, 'Rejoice with me: I have found my lost sheep.' I tell you that in the same way there will be more rejoicing in heaven over one sinner who repents than over ninety-nine righteous persons who do not need to repent."

—LUKE 15:1–7

72

This followed by the parable of the lost coin, where Jesus says:

> Or suppose a woman has ten silver coins and loses one. Does she not light a lamp, sweep the house and search carefully until she finds it? And when she finds it, she calls her friends and neighbors together and says, "Rejoice with me; I have found my lost coin." In the same way, I tell you, there is rejoicing in the presence of the angels of God over one sinner who repents.
>
> —LUKE 15:8–10

Jesus continues with this lesson in the parable of the lost son found in Luke 15. The famous story of the prodigal son should inspire anyone to repent and seek renewal in life when it is needed.

What is clear to me is that when we find something that is lost, we feel good about it. We feel filled with relief and satisfaction. It is nice to know Jesus feels that way when a lost soul returns.

These parables are great stories, and we should all be able to relate to them. They clearly call out to us to repent and to help others find reconciliation with God through repentance. Jesus knew this is not an easy thing for people to do. Not only is it difficult to admit our faults, but it is also hard to change and become committed to a different and righteous way of life. We must, however, persevere with the knowledge that we can be reconciled to God by repenting. Besides an admission of our sin, repentance requires a commitment to correct our ways. Doing so brings joy to heaven where Christ is waiting to open the door to salvation.

FORGIVENESS

For those who repent, the Bible proclaims that forgiveness follows. This is really good news! Likewise, however, we are expected to forgive to those who have wronged us.

Jesus brought to us a clear understanding of this virtue. He teaches us of God's great mercy. In doing so, He set God's forgiveness up as part of God's covenant with us. This covenant includes God's expectation that we'll follow His example.

In Jesus' Sermon on the Mount we have covered His call to us for obedience. In the Beatitudes and the outline of the Law in Matthew chapter 5, Jesus calls us to a very high ethical standard. Yet, knowing our inevitable failure to reach this standard, He calls us to prayer in chapter 6 and ends that theme with a call for us to be forgiving. He says:

> For if you forgive men when they sin against you, your heavenly Father will also forgive you. But if you do not forgive men their sins, your Father will not forgive your sins.
>
> —MATTHEW 6:14–15

In the Book of Mark, Jesus is quoted as saying:

> And when you stand praying, if you hold anything against anyone, forgive him, so that your Father in heaven may forgive you your sins.
>
> —MARK 11:25

Our hope as Christians arises from the fact that our imperfect lives will be forgiven by God, and through His mercy we will be brought into salvation. We rely on this hope and cherish the prospects to which it leads.

Yet, what Jesus tells us is that if we want to count on this virtue of God, we too must possess it. He is telling us there is a link between what God is willing to do and what we are willing to do. In other words, there is a condition that God wants to see us be forgiving before we get His forgiveness. Furthermore, the virtue comes from our spirit and must be manifested in acts of forgiveness by us. Again, we cannot just say we forgive someone. We have to mean it in spirit. Fundamentally, the proof in this virtue is in the living of it.

Jesus cautions us to not judge one another as part of our relationship with others. His words on judgment are an important lesson in our understanding of forgiveness. He says:

> Do not judge, or you too will be judged. For in the same way you judge others, you will be judged, and with the measure you use, it will be measured to you. Why do you look at the speck in your brother's eye and pay no attention to the plank in your own eye? How can you say to your brother, "Let me take the speck out of your eye," when all the time there is a plank in your own eye? You hypocrite, first take the plank out of your own eye, and then you will see clearly to remove the speck from your brother's eye.
>
> —MATTHEW 7:1–5

If we follow these words, we will have less for which to be forgiven. Likewise, to the extent that we can influence others to be less judgmental we will get along better. Christ will judge us all in the end, so our judgment of others is of little consequence. Additionally, we have enough to do trying to get things right ourselves!

Jesus tells His disciples how to handle the sins committed by others, saying:

> If your brother sins against you, go and show him his fault, just between the two of you. If he listens to you, you have won your brother over. But if he will not listen, take one or two others along, so that "every matter may be established by the testimony of two or three witnesses." If he refuses to listen to them, tell it to the church; and if he refuses to listen even to the church, treat him as you would a pagan or a tax collector.
>
> —MATTHEW 18:15–17

In this passage Jesus shares with us His interest in seeing that we pursue reconciliation multiple times and in multiple ways. Yet in the end, if the other party fails to listen, we are essentially to banish them from any further dealings.

Jesus' expectation that forgiveness is, however, endless is confirmed in the following:

> So watch yourselves. If your brother sins, rebuke him, and if he repents, forgive him. If he sins against you seven times in a day, and seven times comes back to you and says, "I repent," forgive him.
>
> —LUKE 17:3–4

Importantly, Jesus tells us that we must forgive each other from the heart. Simply forgiving may be a mental exercise, but that should not be done. Our hearts must be pure and absent of contempt in our forgiveness.

This is easier said than done in many instances. Often I have given forgiveness verbally but taken longer to truly forgive that person in my heart. The thing to remember is that God forgives this way. Thank goodness He does. Some of us keep fouling up and needing forgiveness many times.

As Jesus continued with His ministry, we see a connection between forgiveness and love. This important understanding is clearly related to us in the following:

> Now one of the Pharisees invited Jesus to have dinner with him, so he went to the Pharisee's house and reclined at the table. When a woman who lived in a sinful life in that town learned that Jesus was eating at the Pharisee's house, she brought an alabaster jar of perfume, and as she stood behind him at his feet weeping, she began to wet his feet with her tears. Then she wiped them with her hair, kissed them and poured perfume on them.
>
> When the Pharisee who had invited him saw this, he said to himself, "If this man were a prophet, he would know who is touching him and what kind of woman she is—that she is a sinner."
>
> Jesus answered him, "Simon, I have something to tell you."
>
> "Tell me, teacher," he said.
>
> "Two men owed money to a certain money-lender. One owed him five hundred denarii, and

the other fifty. Neither of them had the money to pay him back, so he canceled the debts of both. Now which of them will love him more?"

Simon replied, "I suppose the one who had the bigger debt canceled."

"You have judged correctly," Jesus said.

Then he turned toward the woman and said to Simon, "Do you see this woman? I came into your house. You did not give me any water for my feet, but she wet my feet with her tears and wiped them with her hair. You did not give me a kiss, but this woman, from the time I entered, has not stopped kissing my feet. You did not put oil on my head, but she has poured perfume on my feet. Therefore, I tell you, her many sins are forgiven— for she loved much. But he who has been forgiven little loves little."

Then Jesus said to her, "Your sins are forgiven."

The other guests began to say among themselves, "Who is this who even forgives sin?"

Jesus said to the woman, "Your faith has saved you; go in peace."

—LUKE 7:36–50

In many respects forgiveness is an extension of love and could easily be a part of the virtue of love. However, Jesus made forgiveness such an important element of His teachings that I felt it deserves to stand as a virtue on its own. Jesus taught us of God's forgiveness, showed great forgiveness to others in His ministry, held out forgiveness to all of us and required us to forgive others in a similar manner.

78

CHARITY

Jesus taught us a great deal on the virtue of charity. Like forgiveness, charity is a form of love that we give to another in need. Nothing should be expected in return, and in its purest form there's never any thought of repayment.

As an expression of a giving spirit, charity to others is a very godlike virtue. Since everything comes from God, and God has mercifully given us all we have, it is only natural that we are expected to share any gifts with those in need. Developing a truly charitable spirit is an important calling for all Christians.

Charity is mentioned often in Jesus' teachings. It is characterized by an act of giving. The record of charitable acts in our lives provides clear evidence of whether we have lived up to Christ's expectations. He will clearly be in a position to judge our acts and the spirit with which we carried out those acts. A record of our charity account is being kept, and for it we are accountable.

In our age of materialism, this virtue is often neglected. Charity requires us to use prudence in what we do with what we have. It calls us to make important choices with the treasures with which we are endowed.

Christ's words call out to us to share what we have. They call us to follow Christ above all our possessions and to not let any possession stand in our way. Charity demands that we be helpful to others in both spirit and deed. Developing that generous spirit and bringing charitable acts to those in need are what this virtue is all about.

In Jesus' Sermon on the Mount He emphasizes good deeds and praising God. He says:

> You are the light of the world. A city on a hill cannot be hidden. Neither do people light a lamp and put it under a bowl. Instead they put it on its stand, and it gives light to everyone in the house. In the same way, let your light shine before men, that they may see your deeds and praise your Father in heaven.
>
> —MATTHEW 5:14–16

This passage does not mean that we should go out of our way to make our good deeds known. But good deeds will provide evidence to the world that the way of the Lord is good. Seeing these good deeds will lead to others to join in the Spirit of the Lord.

Although obedience and forgiveness are also good deeds, we will see that charity calls for action. In fact, if we look at Luke, Jesus very directly speaks about what is needed for a person to be saved. This important story can be found both in Matthew and Mark. In Luke, we are told:

> A certain ruler asked him, "Good teacher, what must I do to inherit eternal life?"
>
> "Why do you call me good?" Jesus answered. "No one is good—except God alone. You know the commandments: 'Do not commit adultery, do not murder, do not steal, do not give false

testimony, honor your father and mother.'"

"All these I have kept since I was a boy," he said.

When Jesus heard this, he said to him, "You still lack one thing. Sell everything you have and give to the poor, and you will have treasure in heaven. Then come, follow me."

When he heard this, he became very sad, because he was a man of great wealth. Jesus looked at him and said, "How hard it is for the rich to enter the kingdom of God! Indeed, it is easier for a camel to go through the eye of a needle than for a rich man to enter the kingdom of God."

—LUKE 18:18–25

Jesus warns that possessions can stand between God and us, but He also directs us to dispose of them to those in need. Having spent much of His ministry teaching, healing and ministering to the weak and the poor, He expects us to do the same. He expects us to reach out and help those in need.

In Luke's Gospel, Jesus, while in the home of a Pharisee, instructs where our heart and actions should be when we want to give to others:

When you give a luncheon or dinner, do not invite your friends, your brothers or relatives, or your rich neighbors; if you do, they may try and invite you back and so you will be repaid. But when you give a banquet, invite the poor, the crippled, the lame, the blind, and you will be blessed. Although they cannot repay you, you will be repaid at the resurrection of the righteous.

—LUKE 14:12–14

The point is that it is important to give to those who cannot repay. To do otherwise is not charity. To give only to those who can repay is simply a form of trading favors. There is no charity involved. Therefore, we are called to seek out those who cannot repay. Charity is giving to those in need who cannot repay. In this same vein, Jesus emphasizes the value of using our resources for others in the Sermon on the Mount, saying:

> Do not store up for yourselves treasure on earth, where moth and rust destroy, and where thieves break in and steal. For where your treasure is, there your heart will be also.
>
> —Matthew 6:19–21

Humility

Jesus taught us humility by His example and by His Word. With all the power in heaven available to Him, He avoided using that power as He went about teaching with grace and truth. He sought not to bring glory to Himself but to God the Father. He resisted bringing attention to many of His miracles, and instead He emphasized the need for spiritual faith.

At the Feast of Tabernacles in Jerusalem, Jesus spoke to a gathering:

> He who speaks on his own does so to gain honor for himself, but he who works for the honor of the one who sent him is a man of truth; there is nothing false about him.
>
> —John 7:18

For people like the Hebrews who were looking for a king to lead them to salvation, these words were far from what they expected. Rather than strength and power, they heard humility.

Even the disciples of Jesus struggled to understand Jesus' teachings of humility. At one point an argument broke out among them as to who would be the greatest disciple. Realizing the true issue, Jesus' reaction is recounted in Luke:

> Jesus, knowing their thoughts, took a little child and had him stand beside him. Then he said to them. "Whoever welcomes this little child in my name welcomes me; and whoever welcomes me welcomes the one who sent me. For he who is least among you all—he is the greatest."
>
> —LUKE 9:47–48

Later in Luke, Jesus told His disciples:

> For everyone who exalts himself will be humbled, and he who humbles himself will be exalted.
>
> —LUKE 18:14

We have all met those who proclaim their own righteousness, their own strength, their own wealth or their own goodness. To these Jesus warns of a coming humbling experience. Yet, those who are humble will be exalted.

Jesus continues to tell His disciples that children have a faith and humility that exemplifies what is expected:

> Let the children come to me, and do not hinder them, for the kingdom of God belongs to such as

these. I tell you the truth, anyone who will not receive the kingdom of God like a little child will never enter it.

—LUKE 18:16–17

Can you remember just how open you were as a kid to the idea of God and Jesus? In some respects you were gullible, but also you were full of faith. Likewise, Jesus expects us to have the same kind of faith and childlike humility.

On another occasion when Jesus was invited to eat at the home of a Pharisee on the Sabbath, He noticed how the guests carefully chose seats of honor at the table. He told them the following:

> When someone invites you to a wedding feast, do not take the place of honor, for a person more distinguished than you may have been invited. If so, the host who invited both of you will come and say to you, "Give this man your seat." Then humiliated, you will have the least important place. But when you are invited, take the lowest place, so that when your host comes, he will say to you, "Friend, move up to a better place." Then you will be honored in the presence of all your fellow guests. For everyone who exalts himself will be humbled, and he who humbles himself will be exalted.
>
> —LUKE 14:8–11

Many people seek the spotlight in group settings. They strive to be in the limelight because it brings them recognition. Yet, Jesus cautions against such an attitude and promotes the opposite.

In another verse Jesus cautions the Pharisees for

their ego:

> Woe to you Pharisees, because you love the most important seats in the synagogues and greetings in the marketplaces.
>
> —LUKE 11:43

Jesus points to those who put themselves in high regard because of their perceived righteousness. He cautions against any boastful claim of righteousness. He emphasizes the mercy and grace given to those who repent and humble themselves before God. This is made clear in the following parable:

> Two men went up to the temple to pray, one a Pharisee and the other a tax collector. The Pharisee stood up and prayed about himself: "God, I thank you that I am not like other men—robbers, evildoers, adulterers—or even like this tax collector. I fast twice a week and give a tenth of all I get."
>
> But the tax collector stood at a distance. He would not even look up to heaven, but beat his breast and said, "God, have mercy on me, a sinner."
>
> I tell you that this man, rather than the other, went home justified before God. For everyone who exalts himself will be humbled, and he who humbles himself will be exalted."
>
> —LUKE 18:10–14

In His teachings Jesus highlights the fact that it is our duty as Christians to serve God. We are not volunteers when we want to be. We are of God, and we are obligated to live according to His will. Our obligation is to live righteously, and all we do should be rendered to God without a selfish claim to anything.

Jesus conveyed this expectation in the following:

> Suppose one of you had a servant plowing or looking after sheep. Would he say to the servant when he comes in from the field, "Come along now and sit down to eat"? Would he not rather say, "Prepare my supper, get yourself ready and wait on me while I eat and drink"? Would he thank the servant because he did what he was told to do? So you also, when you have done everything you were told to do, should say, "We are unworthy servants; we have only done are duty."
>
> —LUKE 17:7–10

As part of our service to God we are expected to give a share of what we earn. We should give this share with thankfulness for the bounty God has given to us. We should give it with no recognition expected or wanted. This Jesus makes clear to us in the following:

> So when you give to the needy, do not announce it with trumpets, as the hypocrites do in the synagogues and on the streets, to be honored by men. I tell you the truth, they have received their reward in full. But when you give to the needy, do not let your left hand know what your right hand is doing, so that your giving may be in secret. Then your Father, who sees what is done in secret will reward you.
>
> —MATTHEW 6:2–4

Here Jesus makes it clear that those who seek recognition for doing good have received their reward. They will not get a reward in heaven for doing it. Only those who shy away from the recognition will actually get credit in heaven.

As part of maintaining a humble presence, Jesus warns us to not judge others. This again reminds us of our duty to pursue God's will by looking to God for judgment. Jesus tells us:

> Do not judge, or you too will be judged. For in the same way you judge others, you will be judged, and with the measure you use, it will be measured to you.
>
> —MATTHEW 7:1–2

Not judging is difficult. It requires that we put God's authority first and then accept our role as a servant in His creation. His will calls us to do as He does and to help others. Jesus summarizes this message in this verse from Matthew:

> So in everything, do to others what you would have them do to you, for this sums up the Law and the Prophets.
>
> —MATTHEW 7:12

Our humility must go to the point of treating others as we would want to be treated. Even in extreme circumstances we are to behave with care for others. Jesus teaches:

> If someone strikes you on the cheek, turn to him the other also. If someone takes your cloak, do not stop him from taking your tunic. Give to everyone who asks you, and if anyone takes what belongs to you, do not demand it back. Do to

others as you would have them do to you.

—LUKE 6:29–31

Boy, this one is tough! The last part works well for me, and I can say that I believe in working on that part is a good and joyful thing. However, the part about turning the other cheek and giving to anyone is tough for me. I have not done this well in my life, and I have room to improve here in a big way.

Turning the other cheek is difficult at times, especially when you know you are right and someone else is wrong. I am a believer in discipline, and I lean toward the big stick mentality to keep peace and discipline in society. I also fear that drug addicts panhandle to finance their unhealthy habit, and I don't want to support that kind of behavior. I love helping those truly in need, but I know my definition of need is not broad enough.

OK, enough about my weaknesses. Jesus teaches us about humility through his miraculous deeds. In the first chapter of the Book of Mark, Jesus heals a man with leprosy, and in sending the man away, Jesus says:

> See that you don't tell this to anyone. But go, show yourself to the priest and offer the sacrifices that Moses commanded for your cleansing as a testimony to them.
>
> —MARK 1:44

Jesus maintained an example of a humble leader who was deeply interested in others to the end. At the end of His life, He died for us, paying the ultimate price of love. Yet, the Jews failed to see the Him as their prophesied Messiah. Adamantly they held to their misguided hope that their Messiah would rescue them politically and place them above all others. Instead, Jesus came to sacrifice Himself for sins and bring us His grace and truth. He gave a divine light for the world to follow. In Him we see humility and an expectation that we follow in that humility.

FAITH

Much of the Old Testament is built around the hope God held for His people. That hope focused on a better land, a better life and a better kingdom ruled by the Messiah. It was an inspiration that has prevailed for generations.

When Jesus came He came as a servant, not as an anointed, almighty king. The Jewish hope anticipated a glorious coming of the Christ. Most of the Jews failed to recognize this servant that walked and taught amongst them. Even when Jesus performed His many recorded miracles, most failed to recognize Him for who He was. Their hope was left unfulfilled even though they were in the presence of the truth and grace of God.

As Jesus went about preaching and teaching, those who followed Him began to realize that He was more than a teacher and prophet. Jesus spoke of God the Father with authority, and He clearly outlined the way to salvation. His message offered to replace the hope of the Old Testament with the faith of the New Testament.

Where hope had held God's people with expectation, Jesus brought us trust that if we believe in Him and do His will we will be rewarded in heaven. He brought us the reassurance of God's love. Furthermore, He told us that through faith in Him we would be delivered from sin.

Following the imprisonment of John the Baptist, Jesus initiated His ministry in Galilee.

> "The time has come," he said. "The kingdom of God is near. Repent and believe the good news!"
>
> —MARK 1:15

We are encouraged to "repent and believe." Repentance is emphasized as a first step to establish with God the fact that we are sinners. With it comes the command to believe in the good news that is the call to faith in Christ the Lord.

God's kingdom with Jesus' presence was so near us at the time of His life that we are alerted to listen and respond to what is coming. The Word of God is given to us, and we are expected to rejoice in it. The importance of the events and the messages delivered were the very cornerstone of the Christian church.

In Luke, the apostles asked Jesus to increase their faith. He replied:

> If you have faith as small as a mustard seed, you can say to this mulberry tree, "Be uprooted and planted in the sea," and it will obey you.
>
> —LUKE 17:6

The disciples were instructed again in the power

of faith when they were near Bethany. Jesus had sought to pick fruit from a fig tree on His way back into the city. With no fruit on the tree, Jesus cursed it with death. It died, intriguing the disciples. Jesus replied:

> I tell you the truth, if you have faith and do not doubt, not only can you do what was done to the fig tree, but also you can say to this mountain, "Go, throw yourself into the sea," and it will be done. If you believe, you will receive whatever you ask for in prayer.
>
> —MATTHEW 21:21–22

Jesus knew it would be difficult for us to develop faith without witnessing miracles that would show His divine powers. He performed many miracles to help us accept the Word and come to be believers. Jesus makes this abundantly clear when He says to a man begging for the healing of his son:

> "Unless you people see miraculous signs and wonders," Jesus told him, "you will never believe."
>
> —JOHN 4:48

While at Capernaum Jesus healed a centurion's servant and commented on the faith of the centurion by saying:

> I tell you, I have not found such great faith even in Israel.
>
> —LUKE 7:9

Again in Luke, Jesus was touched by a woman seeking the healing power of Jesus. He said to her:

Daughter, your faith has healed you. Go in peace.

—LUKE 8:48

In the same town, upon hearing that the synagogue ruler's daughter was dead Jesus is quoted as saying:

Don't be afraid; just believe, and she will be healed.

—LUKE 8:50

Jesus held out the glory of God's kingdom to all believers. In the faith of those who believe in Jesus, He points to the rewards to come. He says:

Rejoice in that day and leap for joy, because great is your reward in heaven.

—LUKE 6:23

Importantly, faith must manifest itself in the doing of good works. Jesus' gift to us does come with obligations. We must use our gifts to do good service. He expects it and judges us on our actions. There is no playing it safe! We cannot remain noncommittal. Faith leads one to do what one can to meet God's will.

Likewise, Jesus makes it clear that it is important to do God's will even if you have very little to work with. In fact, He emphasizes the importance of being faithful in small matters:

Whoever can be trusted with very little can also be trusted with much, and whoever is dishonest with very little will also be dishonest with much. So if you have not been trustworthy in handling worldly wealth, who will trust you with true riches? And if you have not been trustworthy with someone else's property, who will give you property of your own?

—LUKE 16:10–12

In this passage Jesus discusses the value of trustworthiness. He measures trustworthiness even in small matters because it serves as evidence of whether or not one can be trusted with the true riches in heaven. To me, this trustworthiness is part of being faithful.

Next, the faith we have must be backed up with boldness and must be characterized by perseverance. Jesus expects us to be persistent in our service to God. This diligence is discussed when He said:

Be dressed ready for service and keep your lamps burning, like men waiting for their master to return from a wedding banquet, so that when he comes and knocks they can immediately open the door for him. It will be good for those servants whose master finds them watching when he comes. I tell you the truth, he will dress himself to serve, will have them recline at the table and will come and wait on them. It will be good for those servants whose master finds them ready, even if he comes in the second or third watch of the night. But understand this: If the owner of the house had known at what hour the thief was coming, he would not have let his house be broken into. You also must be ready, because the Son of Man will come at an hour when you do not expect him.

—LUKE 12:35–40

Preparedness becomes part of faith. Not knowing when Jesus might return in the Second Coming should cause us to become more prepared, not less. He expects us to be diligent to be ready because it shows faith in Him.

Through faith in Jesus many were healed. Jesus restored sight to a blind man, and He said to the man, "Receive your sight; your faith has healed you" (Luke 18:42).

Yet, Jesus knew that even in the strongest of His followers faith could come and go. When Peter said to Jesus, near the time of Jesus' death, "Even if all fall away, I will not" (Mark 14:29), Jesus responded with the following words:

> "I tell you the truth," Jesus answered, "today— yes, tonight—before the rooster crows twice you yourself will disown me three times."
>
> —MARK 14:30

Peter went on to do just as Jesus had said. The tension and fear surrounding Jesus' capture was too much for Peter. He failed to acknowledge knowing Christ three times that night and was ashamed about it. Yet, in his failure, just as in our own failures, we find Jesus merciful and loving of those who deep in their hearts truly believe in Him.

After His death on the cross, Jesus appeared to the disciples. Thomas was not there, and therefore would not believe what the other disciples had told him. When Jesus appeared, Thomas believed. Jesus said:

Because you have seen me, you have believed;
blessed are those who have not seen and yet have
believed.

—JOHN 20:29

Part of the good news is that as Christians we are
truly blessed because we have not seen Jesus and
still we believe. We live by faith in Him, yet not all
of the time. Often we are like Peter, but we carry
our faith deeply within our hearts, and it keeps
rising up to the surface even when we suppress it
for awhile.

As Jesus approached His terrible death on the
cross, He was in Gethsemane. His prayer there
reflected his ultimate faith in God. He said:

"Abba, Father," he said, "everything is possible
for you. Take this cup from me. Yet not what I
will, but what you will."

—MARK 14:36

In this prayer, Jesus expresses His unwavering
faith in God and His desire to do God's will.
Likewise, we are called to have the same faith to do
God's will.

At times I have wondered if it was easier for
Jesus to have faith because He knew God, He was
from God and He was returning to God. For me,
two thousand years after Jesus' life, it is as though I
have had some of the "doubting Thomas" in me.
My faith has been like the waves in the sea that
Scott likes to surf. It rises and it falls! Yet, as I have
gotten older and learned more, my faith has

increased to the point at which I no longer doubt. Jesus Christ is my Savior!

Fortunately, like Peter's return to faith, most Christians do not stray far without coming back. The Bible is a great record of God's work revealing that Jesus' life is consistent with the records of prophets. Jesus' words ring true. His miracles demonstrate His divine power. His death shows His great mercy and love for mankind. He has blessed many and answered many prayers. Most Christians have sensed His presence and His love. We can only believe, give thanks and have faith to carry on as the friends He has allowed us to be.

As you carry on in faith, you should know that Jesus instructed us on the times in which we live. He emphasizes preparedness so we can miss the tribulation at the end and stand before Jesus as a believer. He says:

> Be always on the watch, and pray that you may be able to escape all that is about to happen, and that you may be able to stand before the Son of Man.
>
> —LUKE 21:36

Our faith in Christ is critical if we want to keep our lives in perspective. It is critical in knowing what is important. It is an essential part of being a true believer.

So keep the faith in God the Father, God the Son and God the Holy Spirit. Pray for the strength to do God's will and rejoice in the rewards to come in heaven.

Preparation

Love

Clearly, Jesus brought love into His ministry. The many miracles He performed were in recognition of an individual's faith out of love for those He touched. He loved those who came to Him to learn and heard the Word of God. He loved those who came in faith to be healed. He loved those who sought His blessing for the need of others. He loved children for their innocence and true faith. He loved those who followed in His path.

In Matthew, Jesus replied to a question asked about the greatest commandment. He said:

> Love the Lord your God with all your heart and with all your soul and with all your mind. This is the first and greatest commandment. And the second is like it: Love your neighbor as yourself. All the Law and the Prophets hang on these two commandments.
>
> —MATTHEW 22:37–40

In both of these commandments, Jesus uses the word *love* as the key verb. He uses this same word throughout His ministry.

Showing the same emphasis, the apostle Paul wrote of spiritual gifts in 1 Corinthians and concludes his discussion with an encouragement to seek the greater gifts. Regarding love, he says:

> Love is patient, love is kind. It does not envy, it does not boast, it is not proud. It is not rude, it is not self-seeking, it is not easily angered, it keeps no record of wrongs. Love does not delight in

97

evil but rejoices with the truth. It always pro-
tects, always trusts, always hopes, always
perseveres.

—1 CORINTHIANS 13:4–7

Of the greater gifts, Paul tells us this:

And now these three remain: faith, hope, and
love. But the greatest of these is love.

—1 CORINTHIANS 13:13

I have noted that the hope of the Old Testament
was replaced with faith in the New Testament. Yet,
Paul assures us that love is the greatest gift!

So the message here is consistent. Love is a
revered virtue that we should all strive to develop
in our Christian lives. But what is this love that
Jesus talks about? Is it the same love we refer to in
passion?

I believe that what Christ speaks of is a deep
sense of caring for others. It is not physical; it is
emotional and spiritual in its existence. It has far
more to do with devotion than it does with affec-
tion.

Anyone can get closer to an understanding of this
love if he has experienced this sense of devotion per-
sonally. To most people it is that sense of belonging
felt among family members. It might be the sense of
close teamwork felt in a sport or a work group.
Often we experience it in that sense of support felt
among close friends.

In addition to our own experience, we can best
understand Christian love from passages in the

Bible. I have chosen a few that collectively should help you understand this virtue better.

Jesus' emphasis on love was highlighted at the Last Supper when He said:

> A new command I give you: Love one another. As I have loved you, so you must love one another. By this all men will know that you are my disciples, if you love one another.
>
> —JOHN 13:34–35

Here Jesus offers Himself as an example of one who loves. He expected the disciples to follow His example and love one another. He knew this then would become an example for those who followed the disciples. As such, it is an example for all Christians to follow.

Jesus' instruction on love comes with some twists. He is very aware of how easy it is for us to accept the notion that we love those with whom we are close, but His Word goes far beyond that. He challenges us to develop a deeper sense of love for one another and to share that love with those we are generally inclined to not love. He tells us:

> You have heard that it was said, "Love your neighbor and hate your enemy." But I tell you: Love your enemies and pray for those who persecute you, that you may be sons of your Father in heaven. He causes his sun to rise on the evil and the good, and sends rains on the righteous and the unrighteous. If you love those who love you, what reward will you get? Are not even the tax collectors doing that? And if you greet only your

brothers, what are you doing more than others? Do not even pagans do that? Be perfect, therefore, as your heavenly Father is perfect.

—MATTHEW 5:43–48

Here Jesus teaches that we are to love those who may not return our love. It is akin to His command for us to be charitable to those who cannot repay us. So it does show how close charity and love are. It also points out the expectation that we serve as an example of love in the world. We can influence those who are evil to convert to good once they experience the love that does exist. It may also influence those who see what is done and come to realize the truth in Christ's way.

In the parable of the Good Samaritan, Jesus brings us closer to an understanding of what is expected in our love for one another. The parable follows:

On one occasion an expert in the law stood up to test Jesus. "Teacher," he asked, "what must I do to inherit eternal life?"

"What is written in the Law?" he replied. "How do you read it?"

He answered: "'Love the Lord your God with all your heart and with all your soul and with all your strength and with all your mind'; and, 'Love your neighbor as yourself.'"

"You have answered correctly," Jesus replied. "Do this and you will live."

But he wanted to justify himself, so he asked Jesus, "And who is my neighbor?"

In reply Jesus said: "A man was going down

from Jerusalem to Jericho, when he fell into the hands of robbers. They stripped him of his clothes, beat him and went away, leaving him half dead. A priest happened to be going down the same road, and when he saw the man, he passed by on the other side. So too, a Levite, when he came to the place and saw him, passed by on the other side. But a Samaritan, as he traveled, came where the man was; and when he saw him, he took pity on him. He went to him and bandaged his wounds, pouring on oil and wine. Then he put the man on his own donkey, took him to an inn and took care of him. The next day he took out two silver coins and gave them to the innkeeper. 'Look after him,' he said, 'and when I return, I will reimburse you for any extra expense you may have.'"

"Which of these three do you think was a neighbor to the man who fell into the hands of robbers?"

The expert in the law replied, "The one who had mercy on him."

Jesus told him, "Go and do likewise."

—LUKE 10:25–37

Again, we see that charity is manifested from love. Our compassion for others is expected to yield an outstretched hand for those in need. Whether we know them or not, whether they are our enemy or not, if they are in need, then we should help.

The story of the Good Samaritan is a well-loved sermon subject. I have heard the story repeatedly since I was a kid. Yet, I have passed up the chance to do this kind of thing for someone else far more often than I have done it, even when I have had nothing but wonderful experiences doing it.

To this day, I can remember some of the people whom I helped when I did not know their names and never heard from them again. I always have been glad I helped them, and I have never regretted doing what I did.

My regrets come from not stopping to help someone I know I could have helped and should have helped. I don't mean the stranded car five lanes over on the freeway. No, I mean the non-threatening homeless person who really needed food, not booze. I mean the ailing person who needed care and I was too busy to stop and help out. I mean the lost person who needed directions to get somewhere and I was just too busy to help.

We are called upon to obey Jesus' word and to follow His example of love. He tells us:

> As the Father has loved me, so have I loved you. Now remain in my love. If you obey my commands, you will remain in my love, just as I have obeyed my Father's commands and remain in his love. I have told you this so that my joy may be in you and that your joy may be complete. My command is this: Love each other as I have loved you. Greater love has no one than this, that he lay down his life for his friends. You are my friends if you do as I command. I no longer call you servants, because a servant does not know his master's business. Instead, I have called you friends, for everything that I learned from my

Father I have made known to you. You did not choose me, but I chose you and appointed you go and bear fruit—fruit that will last. Then the Father will give you whatever you ask in my name. This is my command: Love each other.

—JOHN 15:9–17

Wow! If we do as Jesus commands, we are His friends. Honestly, I have always thought of Christians as being servants to God in the kingdom of heaven. Yet, through Jesus' love He tells us that we are not to see ourselves as servants but rather as friends. As such, we are to consider others as friends in His likeness and strive to love them.

6

CHURCHES

Ken, you asked two questions about the reaction God might have to specific churches. First, you asked, "What might God and Jesus Christ think about the Catholic Church?" Second, you asked, "What might God and Jesus Christ think about the Mormon Church?"

Importantly, whatever God and Jesus think about the questions, you can be certain they think the same thing. Jesus is "in very nature God" (Phil. 2:6), and God has clearly delegated to Jesus the power and authority for judgment over all of us on earth. So, in regards to their answers, they can be considered one and the same answer.

This delegation of judgmental power is very significant, and I will discuss it more in chapter 8 where I answer questions on the tribulation period. For purposes here, let me simply restate a reference to the Book of John where Jesus tells us:

> I am the way and the truth and the life. No one comes to the Father except through me. If you

really knew me, you would know my Father as well. From now on, you do know him and have seen him.

—JOHN 14:6–7

Christianity clearly recognizes Jesus as the Son of God. Therefore, He and God are one and think alike. So God and Jesus will react the same to the actions of people and the work they do through churches.

Now, relative to the broader question, let me first point out that the Scripture tells us that God and Jesus are concerned with us as individuals and as collective members of the body of Christ. There is less concern with which particular church organization we belong. Again, the church they are interested in is the church of the believers in Christ. God did not create all the churches that exist; man did. Since the church age began, with Jesus' commissioning of the disciples after His resurrection, the focus has been on God the Father, God the Son and God the Holy Spirit.

Jesus outlined His great commission to His disciples in Matthew:

> Then the eleven disciples went to Galilee, to the mountain where Jesus had told them to go. When they saw him, they worshiped him; but some doubted. Then Jesus came to them and said, "All authority in heaven and on earth has been given to me. Therefore go and make disciples of all nations, baptizing them in the name of the Father and of the Son and of the Holy Spirit, and teaching them to

obey everything I have commanded you. And surely I am with you always, to the very end of the age."

—MATTHEW 28:16–20

This passage from Matthew was written sometime after Jesus' death. Jesus returned to see the disciples and encouraged them to spread the good news. His charge to them was to baptize and teach. Mark's version is a bit more demanding:

Go into all the world and preach the good news to all creation. Whoever believes and is baptized will be saved, but whoever does not believe will be 'condemned.

—MARK 16:15–16

In starting the church movement, Jesus makes it clear to the disciples that they are to preach the good news. He acknowledges that some will hear the Word and heed it. Those that do will reap salvation. Others will not and will be doomed.

The apostle Paul has written many letters to various churches. In his letter to the Colossians, the apostle makes a very important point about Christ's position in the church. He says:

And he is the head of the body, the church; he is the beginning and the firstborn from among the dead, so that in everything he might have the supremacy.

—COLOSSIANS 1:18

Often Jesus is called the head of the church. The church is often referred to as the body of Christ.

Therefore, Jesus is the head of the body in some references.

John writes of seven different churches in the early portion of the Book of Revelation. All of these churches have different characteristics, and some are viewed more worthy than others. Today there are more churches than I could possibly count. Besides, there are many splinter groups or factions within entire denominations of a single church. These groupings are man-made, not God-made. I believe God sees one Christian church of which Jesus is head.

ONE BODY ON EARTH

Again, it is important to remember that the individual churches within the Christian faith are man-made churches. I will answer your question about specific churches as best I can. In fact, I also will expand on the subject of churches somewhat so as to broaden the answer beyond two denominations. I only ask that you not forget my point about there being one body of Christ, and, hence, one Christian church.

To my knowledge, the Roman Catholic Church is the single largest Christian church in the world. Its membership rolls must approximate a billion people, or one-sixth of the world's population.

Apostolic lineage is an important facet of the Roman Catholic tradition. In other words, they claim a tie exists to their clergy that originates with the disciples. This lineage has been maintained, according to the church and, therefore, gives authority to the Roman Catholic Church above all others.

Catholicism, in and of itself, is a faithful way of living life in commitment to God through Jesus Christ. All Christians share in that responsibility, whether we belong to the Roman Catholic Church, the Protestant churches, the eastern Orthodox churches or any unaffiliated Christian church. We are Christian first and specific church members second.

Tradition says that Peter served as bishop of Rome during his ministry. This position is key to the succession of bishops in the Roman Catholic Church and lends authority to the church as a whole. Although I am not a member of the Roman Catholic Church, I respect the tradition of the church and many of the wonderful things done by church members over the last two thousand years. I consider the members of the church to be Christian brothers and sisters.

The Mormon Church is also called the Church of Jesus Christ of Latter-Day Saints. While the Roman Catholic Church traces its history back to Peter, the Mormon Church is less than two hundred years old. It is often noted for its tradition of polygamy in its early years. Its teachings, however, seem to follow Christ's teachings in ways other than the notorious polygamy, now officially outlawed by the Mormon Church.

Even though there are significant doctrinal

differences between the Mormon Church and main-line Christian churches, the Mormons I have known in my life lead exemplary lives and believe fully in Jesus Christ as the Son of God, His resurrection and His Second Coming. They share a strong sense of family values, and they dedicate substantial time and resources to carry out their ministry. Insofar as they have put their faith in Christ as their Savior, I believe God looks to them as Christians and looks to Jesus to judge them like everyone else.

The membership of all Protestant churches combined is close to half the membership of the Roman Catholic Church. The membership of the Eastern Orthodox Church is smaller still. Many new unaffiliated churches have sprung up throughout the world in recent times. The development of these churches has been important for the Christian movement. As wisdom and understanding grow amongst Christians, the many diverse gifts and cultural expressions within the body of Christ are also given room to grow. These virtues may or may not find the proper structure in one particular church or denomination to allow for their development and use. As such, many new churches that allow and encourage those gifts and expressions come to life and flourish.

To me, this is a natural adaptation of the body of Christ to incorporate the various virtues of all true believers. This is appropriate as long as God the Father, God the Son and God the Holy Spirit remain at the center of our beliefs. The Word of

God is clear on this! It is only followed by the principle commandment to love others as you love yourself. With these commandments in mind, I cannot help but believe that there is a great deal of flexibility in how individuals choose to organize for worship and for doing good works in His name.

APOSTASY

In an opposing view, you should be aware of the concept of "apostasy." Many of the newer churches in our Christian faith believe that apostasy has occurred and is occurring in the traditional churches throughout the world. Apostasy is the backing away from fundamental beliefs while maintaining a false loyalty.

Hence, a very real concern for many Christians is that traditional churches can go through the motions of being Christian while not really being dedicated to the true principles of Christian living. The result is that apostasy leads individuals away from Christ.

Wow, apostasy is a tough and dreadful condition that eats at the core of a person's beliefs or a church's purpose. Although I hear this word more today than ever before in my life, I believe it has been around a long time. Let me explain why.

Protestantism makes up one of the three major branches of the Christian church. During the 1500s, several movements resulted in Protestant churches such as the Lutheran and Anglican churches being formed. These churches rejected the authority of the pope and emphasized the Bible and the individual.

The Orthodox Church formed well before the Protestant movement. However, the reason it formed was a distrust of the Roman Catholic Church hierarchy and a desire to return to more traditional forms of worship. In Eastern Europe, this is the predominant church today.

So, our history as a Christian faith is filled with church division and the birth of new church organizations to meet the collective need of Christians. If these new organizations facilitate the work and worship of Christians, then I believe they are good. If they cause division and focus on hatred, then they are bad. But it is not my place to judge any of them individually. Jesus will do the judging.

All Christian churches must put Jesus Christ at the center of their worship. They need to concentrate on Jesus' teachings and the salvation He offers through His death. They need to encourage good works for those in need.

Although there are faults to be found in all churches, the faults are mankind's faults. They originated from people and are perpetuated by people. Many righteous Christians belong to these churches and follow the will of God. Many worship God with great glory and thanksgiving. Many good works are done in the name of the Lord to spread the gospel and care for those in need by these churches.

Differences exist between many of these churches because there are differences in the membership and differences in the leadership. These differences appeal to people who seek out acceptable ways of displaying their beliefs. Just as members of our family are all Americans, we may still have different political affiliations; the same is true for Christians.

No doubt, there are some ways of church life in one church that bring greater honor to that church. But if we are all Christians, the differences are relatively minor and are not worth quibbling over. What is important is spreading the gospel to increase the number of Christians and encouraging all Christians to do good works for others.

I support this important point with Jesus' own words, where He and John speak:

> "Teacher," said John, "we saw a man driving out demons in your name and we told him to stop, because he was not one of us."
>
> "Do not stop him," Jesus said. "No one who does a miracle in my name can in the next moment say anything bad about me, for whoever is not against us is for us. I tell you the truth, anyone who gives you a cup of water in my name because you belong to Christ will certainly not lose his reward."
>
> —MARK 9:38–41

Therefore, all Christians should be more concerned with themselves and what they do for others than they are with differences in church affiliations. With over half the world non-Christian, we should be spreading the gospel to nonbelievers and not crossing *Ts* and dotting *Is* in internal doctrines. We should be out doing good works for others and not arguing over issues like edifying the local church building. When we work together for one purpose of lifting up the name of Jesus, then we manifest the truth in our faith and our reward awaits us in heaven.

Still, apostasy is a concern. As churches grow old, the fires of faith sometimes diminish to a flickering ember. But in reality, the leadership or the membership becomes lethargic. It loses sight of the true Christian call to action, and so they end up living in a morass of spiritual lifelessness. It may happen to us individually as well as collectively.

Remember, Christianity was founded on the commandments of the Jewish faith and expanded by Jesus who gave His life so that we might live through His sacrifice. Jesus' life of teaching, leading and miraculous healing triumphed in His resurrection, proving His claims of divinity.

Amazingly, the Hebrew people did not accept Jesus as the Son of God. The frustration this engendered in Jesus was enormous. He told them:

> If God were your Father, you would love me, for I came from God and now am here. I have not come on my own; but he sent me. Why is my language not clear to you? Because you are unable to hear what I say. You belong to your father, the devil, and you want to carry out your father's desire. He was a murderer from the beginning, not holding to the truth, for there is no truth in him. When he lies, he speaks his native language, for he

is a liar and the father of lies. Yet because I tell the truth, you do not believe me! Can any of you prove me guilty of sin? If I am telling the truth, why don't you believe me? He who belongs to God hears what God says. The reason you do not hear is that you do not belong to God.

—JOHN 8:42–47

This indictment of the Jewish people who did not believe in Jesus set the stage for their condemnation for years to come. Their exile and persecution continued from the Old Testament era right on into the New Testament era. Even today, they fail to live quietly in peace. Unfortunately according to the Bible, they will have very little peace to look forward to right up to the Second Coming.

Obviously, there are many other religions in the world besides Christianity and the Jewish faith. I want to be careful to follow Paul's lead in not judging those outside the Christian church. In his message to the Corinthians he tells us:

What business is it of mine to judge those outside the church?

—1 CORINTHIANS 5:12

Paul's statement simply recognizes that it is not his role to judge. This is consistent with what Jesus taught, and it is clear from what we have covered so far that Jesus has been given the power to judge everyone. We should not presume to judge in His place. Therefore, I will give you a few brief comments on other religions to help you place them in context with what goes on in the world.

BUDDHISM, ISLAM AND HINDUISM

Buddhism is a religion that incorporates idols. It is focused on Buddha, who lived around the sixth century before Christ. Although it is centered on a virtuous life leading to salvation, it relies on oneself to overcome sin, and it does not recognize the authority of God or the existence of Jesus as His Son. Its major followers reside in China, although there are followers of Buddha throughout the world. Hence, hundreds of millions consider Buddhism their religious focus.

The Islamic faith is followed by more than a billion people today, primarily in the Middle East, Indonesia and northern Africa. It is a religion that embraces many virtues of helping others and is focused on one God, named Allah. Abraham is revered in this religion, and Abraham's son Ishmael provided the family branch for many of the descendants who follow this religion. In Islam, Mohammed, the last prophet in a line of prophets including Jesus, is said to be the one held in highest regard by Allah. Mohammed's revelations and teachings in the Koran, the sacred Muslim book, are reported to be the words of God. However, neither Mohammed, who lived in the 600s after Christ, nor the Islamic religion recognize Jesus as the Son of God.

Hinduism is practiced by hundreds of millions in India and Pakistan. This religion opens itself to a belief in many gods. Idols are used to represent these gods. This religion reminds me in some ways of the old Greek mythology where many gods were involved in the universe. I do not claim to know much of this form of religion, but I know it does not recognize the authority of Jesus as the Son of God.

Still, I know there are millions of faithful people who ascribe to the three religions, who are believers in one God and who do many good works for others. It is my prayer that they hear the Word of God and convert to believe in God's Son, and thereby be saved. As millions have before, and to the extent we can bring the gospel to them, they too can share in the glory of our Lord Jesus Christ. Failure to do so will leave them to endure the wrath of God to come.

Nearly half the population of the world is tied to the spiritual beliefs embodied in these three religions. Where each ties its spiritual belief to many righteous virtues, the focus is either on self, idol gods or false prophets. Traditions and peer pressure have made it difficult for the millions trapped in these faiths to escape and to see the light of the true word from our Lord Jesus Christ.

Then there are a great many people in the world who do not believe in any god. They live for the present and believe there is no large-scale plan for the earth and its people. Many live virtuous lives because of internal morals, but they pay little attention to the possibility of a spiritual world that may offer eternal life. Some live in sin and see no way out. They find religion only an embarrassment to their way of life and, hence, avoid it.

God made us all in His image, and He cares deeply for each one of us. Irrespective of where we are in the world or what church affiliation we currently have, we are all encouraged to participate in one group: the body of Christ. Jesus will judge us, as you have read already and will again read in chapter 8, and it is only through Him that we may be saved to enter heaven. The good news continues to be that those who have true faith in Christ are heaven bound!

7

HEAVEN BOUND

Deidre, you asked two questions about the event called rapture: "Do you believe in pre-tribulation or post tribulation? Do you believe it will happen in our lifetime?"

I believe the rapture will occur before the seven-year tribulation period or early in the period. I also believe it will happen in your lifetime, and hopefully I will be there, too. I believe rapture timing is tied to the tribulation period, which is tied to the Second Coming.

Your questions are similar to those asked by many early church members. Paul was confronted with these questions, and he gives us insight into the answers. I will share these with you shortly.

First, let me note that most Christians thought or hoped for an early return of Jesus. They were, naturally, concerned about what would happen to them. They also wondered what would happen to their Christian relatives who had died recently.

With persecutions continuing for Christians,

those early church members must have felt as the Jews did on many occasions in the past. I can hear their cries to Jesus to not forsake them and to come and rescue them from the tyrannical powers of the times. They shared the same kind of hope held by the Jews for a glorious coming of Christ to justify their faith and to avenge their treatment.

At the same time, many pagan beliefs held that death was the end, whereas Christians held that salvation was there for the taking to everyone through repentance and belief in Jesus Christ. Therefore, knowing about salvation for deceased relatives was important to sustain faith for the Christians.

OK, back to Paul; he teaches two relevant lessons to us in his letters to the Corinthians and the Thessalonians. The first, in his first letter to the Corinthians, he explains that we will be resurrected. Our earthly body will perish and we will be given a heavenly resurrected body. Paul says:

> I declare to you, brothers, that flesh and blood cannot inherit the kingdom of God, nor does the perishable inherit the imperishable. Listen, I tell you a mystery: We will not all sleep, but we will all be changed—in a flash, in the twinkling of an eye, at the last trumpet. For the trumpet will sound, the dead will be raised imperishable, and we will be changed. For the perishable must clothe itself with the imperishable, and the mortal with immortality.
>
> —1 CORINTHIANS 15:50–53

Paul is telling us something here that he calls a "mystery." To me, he is saying this is something that is not ordinary. It cannot be explained in terms that people will understand. It is something special that answers the questions of people, but it is expected to leave doubt in the minds of those who hear it.

Paul goes on to tell us that "we will not all sleep." To me, this is an indication that not all Christians will suffer death. To sleep is to have died, and to be at sleep is awaiting the call from Christ to join Him.

Paul then says we will be changed instantaneously. So, whenever this change occurs, it will happen quickly. I also infer that it will happen to everyone involved at roughly the same time except as noted below. As to when all this happens, I will come back to the timing issue after I cover Paul's second lesson.

The second lesson comes to us in Paul's first letter to the Thessalonians where he responds to questions about the Lord's coming. Paul says:

> According the Lord's own word, we tell you that we who are still alive, who are left to the coming of the Lord, will certainly not precede those who have fallen asleep. For the Lord himself will come down from heaven, with a loud command, with the voice of the archangel and with the trumpet call of God, and the dead in Christ will rise first. After that, we who are still alive and are left will be caught up together with them in the clouds to meet the Lord in the air. And so we will be with the Lord forever.
>
> —1 THESSALONIANS 4:15–17

Paul therefore assures us that the dead and the living believers will be raised, in that order, to become resurrected bodies in Christ. This is commonly referred to as the rapture.

Rapture is a fascinating concept. It is almost fantasy because it is without precedent. Furthermore, the scale of such an event is enormous with mind-boggling consequences for the remaining world. Most Christians struggle to fathom the possibility, and most non-Christians consider it total fantasy. It is a "mystery," as Paul said it would be.

If we agree that Paul is describing the rapture of the church, then we are left with the question of timing. You did not ask for a date on this event, thank goodness, so I simply will try and place it in relation to another event. The question I will answer is, When does the rapture happen relative to the seven-year tribulation?

There are a few statements that clue us in to an answer, but I must admit the answer is not absolutely clear. Most of what I have read on the subject leads one to think the pre-tribulation theory is the correct and merciful interpretation. That is, the rapture occurs before the tribulation period begins and all believers avoid the seven years of judgments. However, I don't see Scripture being totally conclusive that this is the only answer, although I tend to favor it and hope it is right.

First, it is clear that the rapture occurs before the tribulation ends. The evidence is clear that the Lord intends to call Christians at least as early as the first half of the tribulation period. The evidence is in the Book of Revelation. Before John carries through his lengthy description of the tribulation, he quotes the Lord in a message to the church of Philadelphia, saying:

> Since you have kept my command to endure patiently, I will also keep you from the hour of trial that is going to come upon the whole world to test those who live on the earth.
>
> —REVELATION 3:10

Certainly, this leads me to believe that Christians will be called to Jesus before the "hour of trial." Undeniably, the second half of the tribulation is the worst trial ever put to mankind on earth. It is separated from the first half of the tribulation by a short break and a new set of happenings as described further in the Book of Revelation. Hence, rapture must occur before the tribulation or during the first half.

While trying to answer this question I asked myself whether rapture had to happen only once. My early thinking was that it would. Yet, that was only based on my wishful thinking that it would happen before the tribulation so we all would have a chance of missing all of the events associated with tribulation. However, upon objective reflection, I have to admit I have never read in Scripture where rapture will happen only once. As I see it, this is just part of the mystery of which we cannot be certain.

OK, back to timing. Like most people who

consider the subject, I hope the timing precedes the start of the tribulation. And like most people, I do not see where Jesus intends to put righteous believers through the test of tribulation. Just as God spared Lot and his family from the destruction of Sodom and just as God spared Noah from the flood, I believe those who have earned salvation in Christ will be spared the worst of the tribulation. Common sense tells me this is the merciful plan of God and rapture is the means to this end.

Yet, it does not necessarily mean Christians will be spared the entire tribulation. Hoping for it does not make it so. Let me offer the scriptures I found that give evidence of when those who experience the rapture show up in heaven:

In 1 Thessalonians Paul says, "...Jesus, who rescues us from the coming wrath" (1 Thess. 1:10). Rescues usually occur during an event but can occur before the event.

Wrath is first mentioned in Revelation 6, after the seal judgments have been delivered to the world. This takes place during the first half of the tribulation.

At the end of the first series of judgments (i.e., seal judgments) brought to the earth during the first half of the tribulation, the Bible tells us that 144,000 Jews will be sealed by God for protection from the upcoming events of tribulation. John goes on to tell us that he is witness in his vision to a great multitude in white robes who are described as "these are they who have come out of the great tribulation; they have washed their robes and made them white in the blood of the Lamb" (Rev. 7:14).

Later in Revelation John tells us, "I looked, and there before me was a white cloud, and seated on the cloud was one 'like a son of man' with a crown of gold on his head and a sharp sickle in his hand. Then another angel came out of the temple and called in a loud voice to him who was sitting on the cloud, 'Take your sickle and reap, because the time to reap has come, for the harvest of the earth is ripe.' So he who was seated on the cloud swung his sickle over the earth, and the earth was harvested" (Rev. 14:14–16). This is timed at the midpoint of the tribulation and follows the last trumpet of the seven trumpet judgments brought before the midpoint. It involves a harvest of Christians in some form. The rapture is a likely possibility.

The above tells me that Christians are with Jesus by the time the first series of judgments conclude. That is to say they will experience the rapture before or during the early stages of the tribulation. Also, at the midpoint of the tribulation there will be a harvesting that possibly could include the rapture of living Christians.

Beyond this conclusion I find the rest still part of the mystery. I like this conclusion because it fits with the hope that as Christians we will miss the worst of what is to come. It gives those who miss the first rapture a chance to be redeemed in the judgment of Jesus and be spared the horrors of the final half of the tribulation. It also makes some sense out of God's plan.

I see that many people who are close to being believers in Christ may miss the first call to heaven before the tribulation. As such, they will be tested by some of the fire in the tribulation. Such a test will force those near-believers to recognize their mistake, repent and become stronger advocates of Christ. Yet, through their conversion and through Jesus' mercy there is room in the Scriptures to have them join their brothers and sisters in heaven before the worst of the tribulation starts.

The rapture adds balance and transition to the End Times. Jesus spent three and a half years in ministry with the Jews before He died on the cross. This would give Him three and a half years with all Christians in heaven before the end of the age. On earth it provides for a transfer of emphasis from Gentiles to the Hebrew people at the midpoint of the tribulation.

Let me comment on the question of who is called to be with the Lord during rapture. Common sense tells me that Jesus will use the same qualification He will use for salvation.

Naturally, there are those who deserve more reward in heaven for their righteousness and good works. But like the parable of the vineyard owner in Matthew 20 who chooses to pay workers the same wage irrespective of time worked, Jesus may reward all believers with eternal life. Later, each may reap different heavenly rewards according to what they did in their individual lives.

In delivering His just reward to believers, Jesus is preparing a place for us. He tells us of these preparations in John:

> Do not let your hearts be troubled. Trust in God; trust also in me. In my Father's house are many rooms; if it were not so, I would have told you. I am going there to prepare a place for you. And if I go and prepare a place for you, I will come back and take you to be with me that you also may be where I am.
>
> —John 14:1–3

Deidre, I know you have questions about the fate of those who experience tribulation. Although my concept of pretribulation or early tribulation rapture gives comfort to those believers who will be delivered from the worst of tribulation, we sorrow for those who must endure the horrors of the time that follows. The tribulation will be far worse in the second three and a half years.

In Revelation, John tells us what he saw in his vision regarding this time:

> I saw thrones on which were seated those who had been given authority to judge. And I saw the souls of those who had been beheaded because of their testimony for Jesus and because of the word of God. They had not worshiped the beast or his image and had not received his mark on their foreheads or hands. They came to life and reigned with Christ a thousand years. (The rest of the dead did not come to life until the thousand years were ended.)
>
> —Revelation 20:4–5

This tells us that those who resist Satan's plan during the tribulation and turn to Christ will be saved at the Second Coming. This will include millions of Jews and Gentiles who are led to Jesus by the awakening following the rapture, the early tribulation years and by the incredible evangelical movement led by converted Jews. The mercy of the Lord will be upon them, and they will join Him in reigning over the thousand years to follow as noted in chapter 20 of the Book of Revelation.

In summary, the rapture is part of God's mercy for Christians who make it to the tribulation years. It will reward the righteous in Christ and will signal the beginning of the end of the world as we know it.

With hundreds of millions of Christians disappearing at once, the balance of the population will search for an explanation. Many in the world, no doubt, will be led to a false belief by their leaders that the disappearance was a condemning judgment of Christians by God. Many will see through that smoke screen to the truth and stand strong as converted and dedicated Christians. After their trial, they too will join with Christ.

It is critical for us to remember Jesus' words spoken to the Jews who grumbled at His pronouncement that He came down from heaven.

> "Stop grumbling among yourselves," Jesus answered. "No one can come to me unless the Father who sent me draws him, and I will raise him up at the last day. It is written in the Prophets:

'They will all be taught by God.' Everyone who listens to the Father and learns from him comes to me. No one has seen the Father except the one who is from God; only he has seen the Father. I tell you the truth, he who believes has everlasting life. I am the bread of life. Your forefathers ate manna in the desert, yet they died. But here is the bread that comes down from heaven, which a man may eat and not die. I am the living bread that came down from heaven. If anyone eats of this bread, he will live forever. This bread is my flesh, which I will give for the life of the world."

—JOHN 6:43–51

8

JUDGMENT AND TRIBULATION

Karen, you asked, "What happens to those left behind?"

I know you believe Jesus is coming one day to bring salvation to those who believe. Whether there is a rapture before His coming or not, there certainly is a judgment coming—one in which He will judge the future of every soul whether living or dead.

Jesus made it clear that He has been given the authority to judge us. God has given Him the power to choose. The fate of everyone is in His hands.

In answer to the earlier question about for whom Jesus is coming, I noted that He is coming to save those who believe in Him. He is coming to exercise judgment on those who remain. I want to expand on the issue of judgment, so there is no question about Jesus' intent at the Second Coming.

In the book of John, Jesus says:

> Moreover, the Father judges no one, but has

entrusted all judgment to the Son, that all may honor the Son just as they honor the Father. He who does not honor the Son does not honor the Father, who sent him. I tell you the truth, whoever hears my word and believes him who sent me has eternal life and will not be condemned; he has crossed over from death to life.

—JOHN 5:22–24

John the Baptist announced his expectation of Jesus. A description of this is recorded in Luke:

The people were waiting expectantly and were all wondering in their hearts if John might possibly be the Christ. John answered them all, "I baptize you with water. But one more powerful than I will come, the thongs of whose sandals I am not worthy to untie. He will baptize you with the Holy Spirit and with fire. His winnowing fork is in his hand to clear his threshing floor and to gather the wheat into the barn, but he will burn up the chaff with unquenchable fire."

—LUKE 3:15–17

This is the same story told in the Gospels of Matthew, Mark and John. Therefore, it was important to all the disciples. The passage answers why the generation during Jesus' time later thought He might be the Messiah. They easily could have anticipated that this merciful man would show the fire they expected in their Messiah. Today we know He will, but it will be at the time of the Second Coming!

Yet, regarding judgment, in this passage John the Baptist indicates Jesus will separate the good souls from the bad souls. This concept of judgment and separation is repeated many times and is worthy of understanding.

A look at Scripture helps us characterize the judgment process. In Matthew, Jesus tells us:

> But I tell you that men will have to give account on the day of judgment for every careless word they have spoken. For by your words you will be acquitted, and by your words you will be condemned.
>
> —MATTHEW 12:36–37

Therefore, Jesus makes it clear that we render what we believe in what we say. Words serve as evidence of our faith or lack of it. Words demonstrate our love for one another or lack of it. Words are an important part of manifesting our life, and they make up a large part of the record upon which we are to be judged.

Another important parable pertaining to the separation that takes place at the Second Coming is:

> The kingdom of heaven is like a man who sowed good seed in his field. But while everyone was sleeping, his enemy came and sowed weeds among the wheat, and went away. When the wheat sprouted and formed heads, then the weeds also appeared.
>
> The owner's servants came to him and said, "Sir, didn't you sow good seed in your field? Where then did the weeds come from?"
>
> "An enemy did this," he replied.
>
> The servants asked him, "Do you want us to go

and pull them up?"

"No," he answered, "because while you are pulling the weeds, you may root up the wheat with them. Let both grow together until the harvest. At that time I will tell the harvesters: First collect the weeds and tie them in bundles to be burned; then gather the wheat and bring it into my barn."

—MATTHEW 13:24–30

When Jesus was asked by His disciples to explain this parable, He said:

The one who sowed the good seed is the Son of Man. The field is the world, and the good seed stands for the sons of the kingdom. The weeds are the sons of the evil one, and the enemy who sows them is the devil. The harvest is the end of the age, and the harvesters are angels.

As the weeds are pulled up and burned in the fire, so it will be at the end of the age. The Son of Man will send out his angels, and they will weed out of his kingdom everything that causes sin and all who do evil. They will throw them into the fiery furnace, where there will be weeping and gnashing of teeth. Then the righteous will shine like the sun in the kingdom of their Father. He who has ears, let him hear.

—MATTHEW 13:37–43

Angels have been given a huge task of keeping track of all we do. Plus, to do it for every living and dying soul is unimaginable. Yet, the words are clear. Angels are recording what we do and are prepared to assist Jesus in His separation of souls at the time of judgment.

Another parable illustrates the separation of good and evil. Jesus tells us:

> Once again, the kingdom of heaven is like a net that was let down into the lake and caught all kinds of fish. When it was full, the fishermen pulled it up on shore. Then they sat down and collected the good fish in baskets, but threw the bad away. This is how it will be at the end of the age. The angels will come and separate the wicked from the righteous and throw them into the fiery furnace, where there will be weeping and gnashing of teeth.
>
> —MATTHEW 13:47–50

This makes it clear that at the end of time the angels will carry out Jesus' judgment swiftly. Rather than a long drawn out process of judgment, it sounds as if the destiny of those remaining on earth will have been judged, and the angels will separate people based on Jesus' decision.

One of the most famous parables depicting separation is found in Matthew where Jesus tells us:

> When the Son of Man comes in his glory, and all the angels with him, he will sit on his throne in heavenly glory. All nations will be gathered before him, and he will separate the people one from another as a shepherd separates the sheep from the goats. He will put the sheep on his right and the goats on his left.
>
> Then the King will say to those on his right, "Come, you who are blessed by my Father; take your inheritance, the kingdom prepared for you

since the creation of the world. For I was hungry and you gave me something to eat, I was thirsty and you gave me something to drink, I was a stranger and you invited me in, I needed clothes and you clothed me, I was sick and you looked after me, I was in prison and you came to visit me."

Then the righteous will answer him, "Lord, when did we see you hungry and feed you, or thirsty and give you something to drink? When did we see you a stranger and invite you in, or needing clothes and clothe you? When did we see you sick or in prison and go to visit you?"

The King will reply, "I tell you the truth, whatever you did for one of the least of these brothers of mine, you did for me."

Then he will say to those on his left, "Depart from me, you who are cursed, into the eternal fire prepared for the devil and his angels. For I was hungry and you gave me nothing to eat, I was thirsty and you gave me nothing to drink, I was a stranger and you did not invite me in, I needed clothes and you did not clothe me, I was sick and in prison and you did not look after me."

They will also answer, "Lord, when did we see you hungry or thirsty or a stranger or needing clothes or sick or in prison, and did not help you?"

He will reply, "I tell you the truth whatever you did not do for one of the least of these, you did not do for me."

Then they will go away to eternal punishment, but the righteous to eternal life.

—MATTHEW 25:31–46

This passage adds to our understanding of the

judgment process at the end of time. I believe it directly relates to those who are alive at the end of the tribulation, and it may relate to those who have died and not yet received their judgment. But it is clear that Jesus intends to judge souls, and He intends to speak to each group before He sends them to their respective destinations.

I believe Jesus will invoke His power of judgment several times in the future. The first will come to those believers who experience the rapture before the Second Coming. Although the rapture is a form of group judgment, Jesus intends to provide a Day of Judgment for individuals. This, I believe will happen in heaven before the Second Coming.

Paul makes it clear that we must all stand before God in judgment. Two verses give us this expectation. First, in Romans he says:

> For we will all stand before God's judgment seat. It is written: "As surely as I live," says the Lord, "every knee will bow before me; every tongue will confess to God." So then, each of us will give an account of himself to God.
>
> —ROMANS 14:10–12

The second is found in 2 Corinthians, where Paul says:

> For we must all appear before the judgment seat of Christ, that each one may receive what is due him for the things done while in the body, whether good or bad.
>
> —2 CORINTHIANS 5:10

With the assurance that each one of us must stand before Christ in judgment, we can expect this to be done after the rapture. It would seem likely that this would be done before the tribulation is complete when Jesus returns to earth at the Second Coming. Whether it happens just after rapture or after His Second Coming, it will be a time of great reconciliation for all Christians and a bonding time of immense proportions with all our brothers and sisters in Christ.

At the time of the Second Coming, there will be a judgment of enormous proportions brought to those on earth. Many will have been killed during the final battle against Israel just before the Second Coming. Those who survive and, perhaps, those who have died over some time period will be judged as Jesus separates "the sheep from the goats."

Paul tells us of this time:

> God is just: He will pay back trouble to those who trouble you and give relief to you who are troubled, and to us as well. This will happen when the Lord Jesus is revealed from heaven in blazing fire with his powerful angels. He will punish those who do not know God and do not obey the gospel of our Lord Jesus. They will be punished with everlasting destruction and shut out from the presence of the Lord and from the majesty of his power on the day he comes to be glorified in his holy people and to be marveled at among all those who have believed. This includes you, because you

believed our testimony to you.

—2 THESSALONIANS 1:6–10

The seven-year period of the tribulation that precedes the Second Coming will be a period like no other on earth. The entire earth will reel from the events destined to occur. This is the seven-year period of vengeance brought by God on the world before Jesus returns. It has been planned by God for thousands of years at least since early writings in the Old Testament clearly refer to it.

Many books have been written on this period in our future. Some are nonfiction books, providing an interpretation of the Book of Revelation and of the Old Testament prophecies where the tribulation period is symbolically described in detail. Other books are fictitious representations of scenarios that might play out over the seven years.

I leave you to read books of your own selection if this period interests you. I do not pretend to have any special understanding of this period, so I will keep my comments on this period brief and merely highlight some of what is written in the Scripture without doing much interpretation.

What I think you should know are some of the events that are foretold to happen. These are largely from the Book of Revelation and are vaguely interpreted here to give you an idea of the sequence of events. I will not mention the rapture as it was discussed in the preceding chapter.

SEVEN YEARS

Remember that this seven-year period is what ushers in the Second Coming. Critical decisions for the souls of all who live in this period will be made. Each person will have to decide whether he or she stands for the Lord Jesus Christ. There will be no room for middle-of-the-road believers.

Also, the events are so horrible that many will have little time to contemplate the cause and to rationalize what is taking place. Knowledge of the gospel will help many, but those who are focused on the physical changes taking place and not the spiritual cause will suffer unmercifully.

Even those who convert to Christianity during the tribulation, having knowledge and understanding of what is happening, will suffer great pains and loss. Persecution of Christians will escalate through the period; a late conversion will not come without a price!

Keep in mind that many things that happen during the tribulation are destined to happen. Supernatural powers will be used in ways we do not understand to bring it about. Therefore, understanding with natural reasoning will not be helpful. This will be a time period in history when events and their timing will be beyond mankind's control. The only real choices people will have will be whether to believe in Christ Jesus or Satan.

Here are some of the things you will discover if you study the Scriptures, principally the Book of

Revelation:

First 3½ Years

Seven Seal Judgments:

- War, famine and plagues ravage the world.
- Christians are persecuted.
- Earthquakes cause destruction.
- Many Jews come to believe in Jesus Christ.

Seven Trumpet Judgments:

- Fire burns one-third of the earth.
- Volcano/meteor destroys one-third of the sea.
- Meteor poisons one-third of fresh water streams.
- Sun/stars lose one-third of their light.
- There will be five months of locust infestation.
- War kills one-third of earth's population.

Second 3½ Years

Seven Bowl Judgments:

- Antichrist followers suffer pain.
- Sea life dies.
- Fresh water turns to blood.
- Sun scorches everyone.
- Darkness covers the earth.
- Euphrates River dries up.
- Earthquakes/hailstorms occur at Armageddon.

Armageddon is the last event in the list. It is the

name given to the final war in the Middle East where many nations converge to destroy Israel. Jesus' Second Coming is timed to bring an end to the war and begin His kingship on earth for the millennium.

We are still in a time of preparation and expectation of the Second Coming. As I have emphasized before, we should concentrate on strengthening our faith and doing good works. Spreading the gospel and living righteously should be more of our goal than worrying about the events of tribulation. If we believe in Jesus and reach out to help others, we are destined to see the glory of Christ Jesus, who has promised that He has prepared a place for us in heaven.

9

WHEN?

Three of you asked essentially the same question that generations have asked since the prophecies of a glorious coming of the Messiah. When Jesus acknowledged His return, He ignited speculation as to when that return will occur. I cannot help but think that the disciples may have thought it would happen during the remainder of their lives.

Ken, you and Karen asked, "When will the Second Coming take place?" Deidre asked, "Do you believe it will happen in this lifetime?"

I have no idea how many people have attempted to answer this question. Without doubt, there have been many, and most of their predictions have come and gone.

The obvious risk in answering your question is that I would be adding my name to the list. It would be easy to say I do not know. Yet, I will run the risk, for I believe prophecy not only gives us a few clues, but we are now close enough to its fulfillment that we an have a pretty good idea of timing. Things have happened since I was born that make me believe we will see this come to pass in my lifetime.

I caution you, as I have to caution myself, that a preoccupation with the answer to this question can be harmful to your Christian health. There is much work remaining, and it is foolish to worry about the future. I believe it is more important for us to prepare for the coming.

The years ahead of us are important. You and I need to do what we can to assist as many righteous souls as possible to hear the gospel and come to believe in the Lord. In a small way, that is what I am trying to do in answering your questions.

As I have read God's prophetic words over the years, I have come to understand that in giving us these messages God was able to raise hope in those who heard and believed. In times of the Old Testament, believers hoped for land, bounty and salvation. Their hope inspired them and helped them persevere in righteousness. Without hope, righteous people would not have withstood the trials and tribulations they faced.

I believe God wants us to grow in wisdom and understanding. He has transformed Old Testament hope into faith in Christ. Jesus' fulfillment of Scripture during His first coming provides evidence to a true expectation of His Second Coming.

As the time of the Second Coming draws near, I need to dedicate more time to the work of sharing the gospel with those who do not yet believe in

Christ. I don't know quite how to do that yet, but I will work on it. There are still many who need to hear the Word and receive its encouragement.

Although the time between now and the Second Coming is short historically, I do believe we have enough years left to make a difference if we choose to do so. Like you, I will be searching for opportunities and asking God to help me find them.

You have unique gifts, and you should continue to use your individual strengths to do what you can. Even if you don't think you have any gifts or strengths, you can volunteer to help for all sorts of Christian projects. You do not have to give up jobs or relationships. Most volunteers work and find time to help. America is full of folks like this doing wonderful Christian things.

THE END OF THE CHURCH AGE

With this in mind, I will say that God will bring a close to the church age we are in. He has said He would, and He has given us insight into His plan. Knowing you are included should give you great comfort and strengthen your resolve to be a good Christian.

In answering the question of when we can expect the Second Coming, you must first understand that God is the only one who knows exactly when the plan will be carried out. The angels do not know when the Second Coming will take place. Jesus said that even the Son does not know. Jesus makes this clear in His teaching of the disciples on Mount

Olives when He says:

> No one knows about that day or hour, not even the angels in heaven, nor the Son, but only the Father. As it was in the days of Noah, so it will be at the coming of the Son of Man. For in the days before the flood, people were eating and drinking, marrying and giving in marriage, up to the day Noah entered the ark; and they knew nothing about what would happen until the flood came and took them all away. That is how it will be at the coming of the Son of Man. Two men will be in the field; one will be taken and the other will be left. Two women will be grinding with a handmill; one will be taken and the other left.
>
> Therefore, keep watch, because you do not know on what day your Lord will come. But understand this: If the owner of the house had known at what time of night the thief was coming, he would have kept watch and would not have let his house be broken into. So you also must be ready, because the Son of Man will come at an hour when you do not expect him.
>
> Who then is the faithful and wise servant, whom the master has put in charge of the servants in his household to give them their food at the proper time? It will be good for that servant whose master finds him doing so when he returns. I tell you the truth, he will put him in charge of all his possessions. But suppose that servant is wicked and says to himself, "My master is staying away a long time," and he then begins to beat his fellow servants and to eat and drink with drunkards. The master of that servant will come on a day when he does not expect him and at an hour he is not aware of. He will cut him to pieces and

assign him a place with hypocrites, where there will be weeping and gnashing of teeth.

—MATTHEW 24:36–51

Jesus makes it clear that we are to be prepared for the Second Coming. Since judgment will be based on that preparation, I can only emphasize what is written in chapter five of this collection. I do hope preparation comes across as the most important thing Christians can do right now.

In fact, immediately after Jesus spoke the words in the preceding scriptural reference, He goes on to tell us a parable to emphasize this point of preparation:

At that time the kingdom of heaven will be like ten virgins who took their lamps and went out to meet the bridegroom. Five of them were foolish and five were wise. The foolish ones took their lamps but did not take any oil with them. The wise, however, took oil in jars along with their lamps. The bridegroom was a long time in coming, and they all became drowsy and fell asleep.

At midnight the cry rang out: "Here's the bridegroom! Come out to meet him!"

Then all the virgins woke up and trimmed their lamps. The foolish ones said to the wise, "Give us some of your oil; our lamps are going out."

"No," they replied, "there may not be enough for both us and you. Instead, go to those who sell oil and buy some for yourselves."

But while they were on their way to buy the oil, the bridegroom arrived. The virgins who were ready went in with him to the wedding banquet.

And the door was shut.

Later the others also came. "Sir! Sir!" they said. "Open the door for us!"

But he replied, "I tell you the truth, I don't know you."

Therefore keep watch, because you do not know the day or the hour.

—MATTHEW 25:1–13

Jesus tells us that we cannot expect to know the day or the hour. So searching for that detailed an answer would be a big waste of time. Yet, we may know the approximate year.

A less literal interpretation may say that Jesus' words tell us not to seek knowing the answer to when. If you believe that, then you should have no interest in finding out more on this matter and you should stop reading here. On the other hand, if you think understanding more about God's plan will strengthen your resolve as a Christian, then keep on reading.

I think God purposely delivered prophetic messages that included specific timetables throughout the Old Testament to preserve hope and understanding that God has a plan He was following diligently. He did so to prove the accuracy and authority of His Word. Meeting these prophetic timetables strengthened the faith of those who saw them come to pass. So, using the word of God to better understand His plan is OK as long as we keep our priority on doing the preparation work He laid out before us.

Now, understanding this, keep in mind that not everyone needs to interpret the signs of the Second Coming. Nor does everyone need to understand when the Second Coming might happen. Everyone, however, does need to prepare for it!

OK, so much for trying to keep this answer in proper perspective. Let me share some historical and biblical perspectives that I think are relevant. All of this is a buildup to giving you the best answer I can come up with. Keep in mind, Jesus did not give us an answer to your question. Therefore, I am trying to discern the answer from prophecy and common sense. As such, this is a theory on my part.

A THEORY

It is important that you understand that when I answer this question I am giving you a theory. A theory is more than a hypothesis since it is based on the analysis of the facts available. But do understand that the answer is not a prophetic answer because it is not directly from God. Furthermore, I am not a prophet. I am more of a shepherd, and I am simply inspired to use the facts God has given us to determine the best answer I can to your question.

I contend that God's plan reveals some notable patterns of events between the Old Testament and the New Testament. I believe there are many more than I even know about. A few that stand out to me are:

- God's demand that Abraham be

willing to sacrifice his son for God's sake and God's ultimate willingness to sacrifice in the same way through Jesus' death on the cross.

- Reestablishment of a Hebrew nation following exile before Jesus' first coming and later the establishment of Israel in 1948.

- Destruction and restoration of the city of Jerusalem before the first coming and again in the 1500s.

- Persecution of Jews in Babylon before returning to their homeland and the persecution of the Jews in Europe before returning to Israel in 1948.

- The failure of many to see Jesus as the Son of Man when He came and the failure today of many to prepare for His return.

- The time God gave the Hebrew people from Abraham's death to Jesus' coming and the time God is giving the Gentiles from Jesus' death to His Second Coming are virtually the same.

Let me review these important points so you understand them. They lead into the two prophecies that are the only clues I know that relate to the timing of the Second Coming.

Abraham was a key figure in the establishment of the Hebrew people. He gained the respect of God, and God struck a covenant with him that included a promise from God that Abraham's descendants would possess the land we now call Israel. This is the time of a unique relationship between God and the Hebrew people, and it lasted approximately two thousand years up to the time of Christ.

Following Abraham's first covenant with God, he was blessed with a son named Isaac. Later, God tested Abraham's faith by asking Abraham to sacrifice Isaac to God. Abraham was stopped short of that sacrifice, but only after he proved his willingness to carry it out and, thereby, prove his faith. Two thousand years later God sacrificed His Son for our sake, creating a new covenant with all believers in Jesus.

The Hebrew people have gone through many exiles in their history. Their land sits at the crossroads on the east Mediterranean. Importantly, I find that before the first coming, the Hebrew people were in exile in Babylon, and the prophet Ezekiel in the late 500s B.C. prophesied that Israel would be restored. Over the next fifty years he is proven correct. The Hebrew people return to their homeland. Interestingly, in the New Testament era after dispersion throughout the world, the Hebrew people in 1948 returned to a new sovereign country on their homeland.

The third similarity involves the fact that the city of Jerusalem, having been destroyed around 586 B.C., was rebuilt before the first coming, just as prophesied. This occurred after the Persians conquered the Babylonians and allowed the Hebrews to return to their homeland. Yet, after the city was destroyed by the Romans following Jesus' death, it was not rebuilt until the 1500s and has stood since. Daniel, an Old Testament prophet, prophesied a timetable for the first coming from that restoration that is accurate. Using the same timetable to establish a date for the Second Coming is something I will share shortly.

The fourth similarity in time periods involves persecution. Persecution is something that is synonymous with the Jewish people. They have been on the receiving end of persecution for much of their history as a people. Only after severe persecution in Babylon did they get a chance to return to their homeland. Likewise, only after severe persecution at the hand of Germans did they get to return home after World War II.

Christians have had their share of persecution over the last two thousand years, but the knowledge of Christ and faith in Him have enabled us to overcome all of the persecution. Unfortunately, just as many people did not see Jesus for who He really was while He was among us two thousand years ago, many still do not see or feel His presence in the world today. We can pray for their salvation and do such works as to show them the way to righteousness.

The fifth similarity between the Old and New Testaments involves the failings of the Jewish people to recognize Jesus' first coming and His Second Coming. Although prophecy witnessed to the fact He would come as He did two thousand years ago, He was not accepted for it. Today, after all that has been written and all that has happened, the Jewish people still fail to recognize Jesus as the Son of God.

The sixth similarity involves the balance God has provided in His plan for the Jewish people and the non-Jewish people. The time from Abraham's death until Jesus' birth is approximately 1,986 years. God has allowed the church age to exist 1,971 years since Jesus' resurrection. So, the balance in time is remarkable.

THE JEWISH PEOPLE

The last point I want to make, before I move on to the specific prophecies involving when we can expect the Second Coming, has to do with the Jewish people and their overall history. It is amazing when you think about the defeats, the exiles and the persecutions that the Jews have undergone that they even exist as a people. They are the most resilient people in the history of the world, and I cannot help but believe that they have special protection from God.

No other small nation that I know of has withstood all the peril they have and survived. I have to believe the covenants made with God, as recorded in the Bible, stand.

With the similarities in events between the two Testament periods fairly evident to me, I come to the two biblical prophecies that I believe reveal the approximate time when the Second Coming will happen. The first of these is from the prophet Daniel in the Old Testament.

If you remember in answer to Karen's question on the signs of the Second Coming, I quoted Daniel chapter 9 where Daniel is told seventy "sevens" are decreed for six things to be carried out. Daniel writes:

> Know and understand this: From the issuing of the decree to restore and rebuild Jerusalem until the Anointed One, the ruler, comes, there will be seven "sevens," and sixty-two "sevens."
>
> —DANIEL 9:25

I believe the Anointed One is Jesus. If you read Acts 10:38, I think you can see my logic. Also, it is widely accepted that the "sevens" refer to periods of time extending seven years. So, seven 'sevens' equals a time period of forty-nine years. Likewise, sixty-two 'sevens' equates to 434 years. I will come back to the timeline shortly.

Daniel goes on in the very next verse to tell us the event involving Jesus to which he is relating.

> After the sixty-two "sevens," the Anointed One will be cut off and will have nothing. The people of the ruler who will come will destroy the city

and the sanctuary. The end will come like a flood: War will continue until the end, and desolations have been decreed.

—DANIEL 9:26

To me, this verse refers to the time of the end of Jesus' ministry. It tells us that Satan, the ruler of the people, will bring about war until the End Times when "desolations" are decreed, and the end occurs quickly like the times of Noah. Sounds a lot like the tribulation period that follows the church era! In fact, the very next verse is conclusive to me that Daniel's vision relates to the tribulation, where he outlines a seven-year period at the end that matches the description in Revelation. Daniel says:

He will confirm a covenant with many for one "seven." In the middle of the "seven" he will put an end to sacrifice and offering. And on a wing of the temple, he will set up an abomination that causes desolation, until the end that is decreed is poured out on him.

—DANIEL 9:27

So let's look at these verses. In this vision, Daniel is told in quantifiable terms the period from a specific event to the time of Christ. Again, keep in mind the prophecy is written around 165 B.C. Daniel does not have any knowledge of the first coming, much less the Second Coming.

I believe Daniel's prophecy relates to two periods of time. Once in the Old Testament leading up to the first coming. Second, I believe it relates to the New Testament period leading up to the Second

Coming.

Interestingly, in 444 B.C. Nehemiah, a Jew, left exile with the blessing of the Persian king to become governor of the region around Jerusalem. He helped the Hebrew people rebuild the city with emphasis on rebuilding the walls around the city. The walls were rebuilt under Nehemiah's direction in according to Nehemiah's own record in chapter 2 of his book in the Bible.

This leaves a period of time of 474 years between Nehemiah's restoration work and the death of Jesus, or the "cutting off of the Anointed One." Since biblical years are based on the Hebrew calendar, we know a year on that calendar was different from the 365-1/4 days we now use. Our home encyclopedia says this about the Hebrew calendar:

The ancient Hebrews were not very interested in astronomical studies and seem to have adopted their empirical lunisolar calendar from that of their Babylonian neighbors. The months in the Jewish calendar were either full (30 days) or deficient (29 days) and were regulated as much as possible by lunar events. Intercalations were, for a long time, arbitrarily decided upon by government authorities or, in the first 3 centuries A.D., by the Sanhedrin.[1]

This likely reconciles all the difference between sixty-nine "sevens" today vs. a biblical sixty-nine "sevens." So, it seems the sixty-nine "sevens" is equivalent to 474 years today.

Now, if we apply this prophetic timetable to the

New Testament, guess what? Researching this issue, I find that it is a well-known fact that the walls surrounding Jerusalem were destroyed shortly after Jesus' death. What is not so well known is that they remained that way until the time of the Ottoman Empire in the 1500s. In 1536, Suleiman the Magnificent began construction of the wall surrounding the City of Jerusalem.[2]

Using the 474-year timeframe for Daniel's sixty-nine weeks of years, I get 2010 as the approximate date for the end of the church age and the beginning of the tribulation period. This leads to the conclusion that the Second Coming occurs in approximately 2017.

If God wanted the time of Daniel to stop after the sixty-nine weeks of seven years for the Jewish people and replays that time period for the Gentiles in a similar manner, then this theory may be right. It also falls in the same general timeframe for the Jewish people from Abraham to Jesus as it is for the Gentiles from Jesus' first coming to the Second Coming.

The New International Version Study Bible includes a chronology of biblical events. The time period between Abraham's death and Jesus' birth is shown to be approximately 1986 years. The time period between Jesus' death and His Second Coming I have theorized is 1987 years. Not exactly the same difference, but it is an intriguing coincidence that shows a degree of relative balance in what God may have allowed for both the Jewish people and the Christian church.

If Daniel provided the only prophecy on which to draw the conclusion that the Second Coming would occur in approximately 2017, then I would say it is a bit of a stretch to support that position. Yet, the balance of time point I made above draws me closer to seeing the relevance in 2017. Still, I felt it was necessary to look to see if there was another fact that substantiates this conclusion because my account of Daniel's prophecy may not be properly interpreted.

What follows is a quote from Jesus:

> I tell you the truth, this generation will not pass away until all these things have happened.
> —MATTHEW 24:34

This verse follows Jesus' description of what we will see at the coming of the Son of Man. It follows His description of the tribulation times.

OK, what is meant by the verse, and how can we relate it? Well, a generation is frequently considered to be at least seventy years in the Bible. Moses describes a generation to be seventy to eighty years in Psalm 90:10. Yet, Matthew 1:17 indicates that at Jesus' time a generation is considered to be seventy years because that is nearly the exact time noted for fourteen generations between Abraham (died in 1991 B.C.) and David (born in 1010 B.C.).

Importantly, Jesus' statement is part of His answer as to what the disciples can expect at the end of times. He warns of war, famine and earthquakes. He warns of persecution, false prophets and so forth. But what generation is He referring to?

Since He was talking to the disciples, it is as though they are part of the last generation and they should expect to see all these things occur in their lifetime. Yet, we know that was not true, so there must be another generation to which this applies.

For God to have all that is planned for the Jewish people in the tribulation period to happen, it seems that they have to be in control of their homeland and, particularly, Jerusalem. Until 1948 that situation was not in place. Since 1948, and more so since 1967 when the Israelis expanded their territory, the Jews controlled their homeland.

If a generation can be considered to be "seventy years" (which is sixty-nine years using the same calendar adjustment), then the Jewish people will have had a full generation in their homeland by 2017. The expectation of the Second Coming in 2017 coincides with that generation.

Now, I admit that I do not know if this is exactly the generation that Jesus is referring to in His prophecy. I do believe that 1948 represents the New Testament fulfillment of Ezekiel's following prophecy:

> For I will take you out of the nations; I will gather you from all the countries and bring you back into your own land.
>
> —Ezekiel 36:24

The reestablishment of Israel as a nation set the

stage for the end of the Gentile church age. It opens the door for the next great events to unfold. Whether the timeline I outline is approximately correct or just coincidental, the events will truly unfold as prophesied. We need to be patient and be prepared as we wait for the time of the Lord.

I hope this sheds light on a difficult subject in religious prophecy. I pray your understanding increases as well as your commitment to help others. May God bless you in your service to Him!

10

CLOSING COMMENTS

Karen, Ken, Deidre and Scott, when I asked you to give me any questions you had on the Second Coming of our Lord Jesus Christ, I did not know what kind of questions to expect. For certain, I did not know all of the answers and could not have adequately handled the questions in a family room chat.

Your questions were thoughtful and deep. I hope the answers over which I have labored will help you to form the answers you will live with in the years ahead. Your answers do not have to be the same as mine. I only hope my work inspires you and helps you reach your answers. For certain the questions each of you asked are important, and therefore, the answers are important.

With all the day-to-day activities life brings our way, putting our beliefs in order will help ensure our actions are pointed in the right direction. And I do not mean that we will always go in the right direction. We all have a little of the prodigal son in us. Yet, we should always give thanks for all our blessings, whatever they may be, and keep asking for strength to do God's will.

Each of you is going in directions led by your heart and mind. It is good to know that you are in control of those things that will be important to you always. Your beliefs are yours, and no one can change those. The good and bad events you experience in life are merely opportunities to manifest your beliefs. I hope you continue to take control and ownership of your beliefs and let them guide your lives.

I know that over the years I occasionally felt that I was not in control of either what I was doing or who I was becoming. In every case, the barriers I saw were ones I created myself, even though I thought someone or something else was to blame. So, when I recovered to the point of realizing that it was a self-imposed barrier, I got back in control and felt better about myself. Praying for help has always been an integral part of working through such times, and I highly recommend it.

Times do change, and we all face different challenges. It is interesting to note that my father grew up through the depression of the 1920s. He learned to be frugal and still enjoyed those years in West Texas. After becoming an aviator, he found himself in the Philippines in the early stages of World War II. After escaping the invasion, he worked his way to the Dutch East Indies, where he met his future bride-to-be. Then he was captured on his way to Australia.

Imagine being twenty-three years old and having to spend three and a half years in prison in Singapore, Japan and China. The brutality of life was a cruel reality for your grandfather. He was fortunate to survive, to recover and to enjoy a full career and life.

As I grew up I often reflected on how good things were for me. Then one day the draft board came after me to fill their quotas for the Vietnam War. Fortunately, I was allowed to finish my engineering degree and serve my military time as an Air Force officer. But the thought of not being able to control where I lived and what I was to do was real, like my father's. He had to suffer through the horrors of being a prisoner in hell ships and concentration camps in the Pacific. I was more fortunate.

You have not had your lives threatened with overwhelming outside forces that disrupt the basic freedom you enjoy. For that I am thankful!

Yet, in recent times you have seen the terror of war strike our homeland with the September 11, 2001 attacks on New York City and Washington, D.C. These attacks were followed by others acts of terrorism and show the kind of hate some people have for others. Those that become possessed to carry out such acts are far removed from the teachings of our Christian faith.

This kind of vengeful behavior can only reinforce my belief that during the tribulation period people will be capable of committing many horrible acts. The wrath of God will be upon them and their condemnation awaits them. Unfortunately, they influence countless others to do as they do or threaten them with death if they fail to be supportive. Many innocent people are victims of being led to evil in all parts of the world.

In fact, many people throughout the world suffer this lack of control over their lives. Countless numbers of people are suffering brutality. In many places, people lack the basic necessities of life and are forced to spend their entire day pursuing existence. Finding food, water, clothing and shelter still consumes the lives of untold millions.

You are blessed with what you have, and you have far more control of your life than most. You should be well prepared for the Lord!

Anyone in the world can seek that same kind of control if they open their minds, hearts and souls to the Word of God. Besides the wonderment of God's love for us, He has outlined a plan where the righteousness of Jesus prevails over the evil.

Just as we have learned that Jesus will make His Second Coming in glory, we are assured that in the interim we are part of God's plan. God wanted us to have the opportunity to live our lives on earth and to take it upon ourselves to choose righteousness over evil. He is providing us time and spiritual guidance in the process as noted by Jesus, when He said:

> But I tell you the truth: It is for your good that I am going away. Unless I go away, the Counselor

will not come to you; but if I go, I will send him to
you. When he comes, he will convict the world of
guilt in regard to sin and righteousness and judgment: in regard to sin, because men do not believe
in me; in regard to righteousness, because I am
going to the Father, where you can see me no
longer; and in regard to judgment, because the
prince of this world now stands condemned.

I have much more to say to you, more than you
can now bear. But when he, the Spirit of truth,
comes he will guide you into all truth. He will not
speak on his own; he will speak only what he
hears, and he will tell you what is yet to come. He
will bring glory to me by taking from what is mine
and making it known to you. All that belongs to
the Father is mine. That is why I said the Spirit will
take from what is mine and make it known to you.
In a little while you will see me no more, and then
after a little while you will see me.

—JOHN 16:7–16

We are largely unaware of the enormous spiritual battle that exists in heaven. We are but a
battlefield in that conflict. We only know that a
great battle exists between God and Satan, a fallen
angel from God's very own throne. Our lives are
part of God's plan to deal with Satan because
Satan challenged God's creation from the time of
Adam and Eve.

Yet, Jesus' life has been sacrificed for our ultimate salvation, and that is the great news in God's
plan. Jesus will carry out God's will on Satan and
on all his followers at a time appointed by God.
Blessedly, God has told us what we need to know

about His plan. Now we must have faith in His Son Jesus Christ and carry on doing the work He has given us to do.

As part of that work, we know the gospel continues to be spread across the world by Christians. We know that good works are in progress every day. We must do what we can to spread the light of Christ in what we say and in what we do. Jesus told the disciples the following:

> No one lights a lamp and hides it in a jar or puts it under a bed. Instead, he puts it on a stand, so that those who come in see the light. For there is nothing hidden that will not be disclosed, and nothing concealed that will not be known or brought out into the open.
>
> —LUKE 8:16–17

I know that I have more to do. I do not know how I will do it. I only know I want to help others in their journey to Christ. Perhaps putting these words down for you is the next step for me. Thank you for the questions! May God bless you always, and may He give you the Christian faith and love to bless others!

—LOVE, DAD

NOTES

CHAPTER 9: WHEN?

1. David J. Goldberg and John D. Rayner, *The Jewish People* (Viking Publishing, 1987).
2. Judah Gribetz, *The Timetables of Jewish History* (New York: Simon & Schuster, 1993), 169.

To contact the author:

Rob Michie
1410 Westview Place N.W.
Olympia, WA 98502

Email: michieclan@aol.com